Advance praise for
The M Word

Lori Sackler's advice on overcoming the money taboo will not only help families successfully transfer wealth and deal with all of life's transitions, but actually become happier in the process.

Shawn Achor
Author of the international bestseller
The Happiness Advantage

With extraordinary insight, wit, wisdom, emotional intelligence, and practicality, Lori Sackler here masterfully delivers honest, timeless, and highly useful guidance that will help investors and their families successfully navigate crucial life transitions and financial decisions. There is something for everyone in this brilliant book.

David M. Darst, CFA
Chief Investment Strategist
Morgan Stanley Wealth Management

There are few financial advisors as aware of the psychological and emotional issues that accompany family wealth as Lori Sackler. *The M Word* should be on the bookshelf of every parent looking for guidance on how to talk to the next generation about money.

Eileen Gallo, PhD, and Jon Gallo
Authors of *Silver Spoon Kids: How Successful Parents Raise Responsible Children*
and *The Financially Intelligent Parent: 8 Steps to Raising Successful,*
Generous, Responsible Children

Few people give advice as sound as Lori Sackler. *The M Word* will take you by the hand and give you what it takes to survive and thrive financially during these trying times.

Joan Hamburg
WOR Radio

The words "wealth management" are way overused in our industry. Most people think it relates only to how a portfolio is managed and what kind of return you can generate. This book goes way beyond how to manage a portfolio and gets into virtually every financial challenge one may need to be prepared to deal with in their lifetime. The use of real-life examples makes the book even more compelling. Importantly, it also addresses the elephant in the room around most people's financial planning: getting the entire family involved. A great book for every member of the family.

Charlie Johnston
Former President
Morgan Stanley Smith Barney

Money is a difficult topic for any family to discuss, whether it involves marriage, caring for family members, retirement, or estate transfers. Lori Sackler provides many insights about how families can cope with the financial dimensions of what she calls "life's transitions." Her wealth of experience working with families is evident throughout her new book, *The M Word*.

Richard C. Marston
James R.F. Guy Professor of Finance, Wharton School
Director of Wharton's Private Wealth Management Program

Lori Sackler gets that people really struggle to talk about finances *and* that failure to talk leads to much relationship angst. She has taken her vast experience and sensitivity and put it in an excellent guide to money communication and management. Families can spare themselves a lot of heartache by reading it.

Gail Saltz, MD
Clinical Associate Professor of Psychiatry,
The New York Presbyterian Hospital
Today Show contributor

Most financial planning books breeze over or ignore the really tough money decisions. Not this book. It tackles all of life's major challenges to help you really plan your financial future, not just dream about it. Most financial planning books are targeted to the average household and never touch upon the subjects that are vital to you as your wealth level increases. *The M Word* goes the extra mile. The average American won't have a meeting with a wealth manager, CPA, and estate attorney, but as your wealth increases, that is one of the most important steps you can take to secure your future. I'm ordering books for my sons and stepsons so we can have the "Money Talk" Lori's book encourages.

Martin M. Shenkman
CPA, MBA, PFS, AEP (distinguished), JD, Estate Planning Attorney,
and Author of 42 books on estate and related planning

Talk Me the Money! With insight and information, Lori Sackler in *The M Word* teaches us how to have essential, productive conversations about our financial anxieties and goals that will enhance our financial well being. Written in an engaging style with plenty of examples, *The M Word* is Must reading!

Hendrie Weisinger, PhD
Author of *The Emotionally Intelligent Financial Advisor* and
Nerves of Steel: 21 Strategies for the Age of Pressure

The M Word

The
MONEY TALK
Every Family Needs to
Have About Wealth and
Their Financial Future

LORI R. SACKLER
WITH TODDI GUTNER

New York Chicago San Francisco Lisbon London Madrid Mexico City
Milan New Delhi San Juan Seoul Singapore Sydney Toronto

1 2 3 4 5 6 7 8 9 0   QFR/QFR   1 8 7 6 5 4 3

ISBN 978-0-07-179983-6
MHID 0-07-179983-4

e-ISBN 978-0-07-179984-3
e-MHID 0-07-179984-2

McGraw-Hill Education books are available at special quantity discounts to use as premiums and sales promotions or for use in corporate training programs. To contact a representative, please e-mail us at bulksales@mcgraw-hill.com.

This book is printed on acid-free paper.

Library of Congress Cataloging-in-Publication Data

Sackler, Lori.
  The M word : the money talk every family needs to have about wealth and their financial future / by Lori Sackler. — 1 Edition.
    pages cm
  ISBN 978-0-07-179983-6 (alk. paper) — ISBN 0-07-179983-4 (alk. paper) 1. Finance, Personal. I. Title.
  HG179.S23 2013
  332.024—dc23
                                                                    2012043778

Contents

Acknowledgments

Hillary Clinton popularized the phrase, "It takes a village to raise a child" by using it as the title for her internationally acclaimed book. I have learned that tackling tough tasks requires the support and help of a number of wonderful and talented people. It took a village, or what I call my A team, to write this book. Many people I have spoken to along the journey say that writing a book is like giving birth. In this case, it was a particularly apt metaphor, given that from the time I signed the contract, I had nine months to deliver a manuscript to the publisher. I would not have been able to meet that deadline and bring my M Word vision and mission to fruition without each person who helped me along the way. I want to recognize them publicly and express my deepest gratitude.

First, I want to thank my clients for the privilege and joy of working with them over the years. They are ultimately responsible for the insight, knowledge, and personal quest that led to the creation of my radio show and this book.

Thanks to my friends Saranne Rothberg and Leigh Anne Brodsky, who recognized the merit in my message and served as mentors in the early stages of the development of the M Word concept and the radio show. My friends at WOR radio, Jen Buckley, Dawn Ellison, and Jared Lapin, helped me launch *The M Word* on the radio waves and were supportive and flexible as I carved out an evolving message over a three-year period. The primary producer of the show, the amazing radio guru Shelly Gonshorowsky, was a joy to work with and a true friend. Jane Hewson, with her kind heart and energetic mind, served as a producer for a period of time and helped shape the vision and organization of this book. Jocelyn Rosenberg jumped in as producer for the second season and showed a wonderful flair for the subject matter.

There were a number of extremely knowledgeable and sophisticated friends and financial and estate professionals whom I interviewed for the book whose insights were critical to the content and the message. Those who agreed to be mentioned are Manny Canales, James Cotto, Vijay Dalal, David Darst, Mel Konner, Tracy Lee, Patrick Manion, Nancy Monmarquet, Michael A. Murphy, Rebecca Powell, Gary Press, Dr. Jeffrey Rossman, Dr. Richard Sackler, Dr. Joseph Schlessinger, Dina Schwartz, and Martin Shenkman.

My seasoned literary agent, Leah Spiro, is the reason this book became a reality. She was committed to the project early on, was instrumental in securing McGraw-Hill as the publisher and, luckily for the team, contributed her editing experience and talents along the way. My collaborator, Toddi Gutner, a smart and gifted personal finance writer, brought her more than 20 years of writing experience to the project, as well as an unwavering dedication to the topic. My warm and savvy publicist, Meryl Moss, was of immeasurable help in spreading *The M Word* so that it could reach the audience that would most benefit from it. And I would like to offer special thanks to Mark Levine, who guided me through the process with his wisdom, experience, and magic as an editor, writer, and amateur psychologist.

I want to thank the talented and dedicated team at McGraw-Hill who steered me through the process and helped make a long-held dream a reality: Pattie Amoroso, Jennifer Ashkenazy, Mary Glenn, Cheryl Hudson, and Lydia Rinaldi.

I have to acknowledge with sincere gratitude the team of professionals and managers at Morgan Stanley Wealth Management, without whose support and commitment of time and talent the book would have never been published or reached so many people. They are Charlie Johnston, Les Klein, James Wiggens, Tricia Nestfield, Glenn Kurlander, Rick Skae, Drew Hawkins, John Campbell, Rick Donovan, Richard Less, Edward Buecker, Kevin Fitzgerald, Rick Apicella, Mark De Angelis, Kate Festa, Ardell Roan, Ana Mompellier, and Nancy Hecker.

I have had some serious health challenges in the past several years, but thanks to my amazing medical A team of traditional, integrative, and alternative practitioners, I was able to sustain my energy and successfully manage my health throughout the writing of the book. I want to thank Dr. Cynthia Geyer at Canyon Ranch, Dr. Isadora Guggenheim, Dr. Robin Leder, Dr. Austin Pattner, and their staffs.

Finally, I have a lovely and loving family that I adore and rely on for daily strength and sustenance. My husband has been my greatest fan and the most trusted friend and advisor in my life. During the process of writing this book, he provided humor and balance when I needed it and spent considerable time reading and reviewing chapters, helping me stay on course. I will be forever grateful for his unwavering support of the project and his confidence in me as I and my team muddled through the arduous task of writing. And thanks to my sons, Henry and Eliot, who always keep me grounded and humble and who provided much of the inspiration for my wanting to make a difference by writing the book.

Lori Sackler

Introduction

In my family, the "M Word" was not something that was openly discussed. Money was not a topic of conversation at the dinner table or talked about one-on-one for educational or informational purposes. The subject, which was "taboo," was a regular source of conflict and mystery at the same time. Sometimes I overheard my parents speculating as to how well or poorly certain friends and family members were doing financially, but even then it was all very vague and not substantive. The only open and clear Money Talk I heard when I was growing up was from my father, a prominent Dallas urologist, regularly lamenting that my mother, a kind, charming, and devoted wife, mother, and community volunteer, was spending too much of it, and that he was under considerable pressure to keep up with the family's cash flow requirements.

While I admired my mother tremendously, I saw that her fate was undeniably tied to my father's because of her financial dependence on him. Like so many women of her generation, she had abdicated financial control to her husband and had not considered the option of pursuing a career of her own. I resolved to be a different kind of woman: a woman who was in charge of her own destiny. I wanted to be financially astute and not rely on anyone else to make my money decisions. That led me to pursue a career in finance and to obtain a Certified Public Accountant license, then a Certified Financial Planner designation, and finally a Certified Investment Management Analyst designation.

In my role as a financial advisor, it became more and more apparent to me that, as in my own family, the discussion of money in my clients' families was often nonexistent. I began to see where, how, and why family relationships were disrupted and sometimes torn apart because there hadn't been proper communication and planning concerning financial matters. Because I was the financial advisor, I was often caught in the middle of these family blowups. Family members would get angry with me when the real culprit was the lack of communication and trust that was feeding the family meltdowns. These frustrating situations went on for several years. While I sought guidance, I could not find a template for how to successfully affect or change these family situations.

Then in 2003 I attended a Certified Investment Management Analyst conference in Washington, DC, sponsored by the Investment Management Consulting Association. It was there that I first heard Roy Williams and Vic Preisser speak about their new book, *Preparing Heirs: Five Steps to a Successful Transition of Family Wealth and Values*. I heard about the relatively low percentage of families that successfully transfer wealth across generations. Of course, I had already experienced that reality in my own practice, and I had worked with my clients to make sure that they were part of the successful minority. But what was so enlightening was learning that it was primarily the breakdown of communication and trust that caused these families to fail.

A lightbulb came on. Williams and Preisser had actually provided me with a larger context, an explanation, and a potential solution to a problem that I had been experiencing in my wealth-management practice and observing personally with friends and members of my extended family. I knew that Williams and Preisser were providing important insights. I was in the trenches working with families and seeing the enormous problems firsthand, and now I had the foundation I needed to formulate a response that could be meaningful to my family members and clients.

The more I read, the more I was shocked by the enormousness of the problem of families not communicating about financial issues. I began to read everything I could find on the topic to develop tools that would help to guide families successfully through money transitions. I learned that the topic was not simply an American problem: Similar trends and failure rates have been observed internationally as well. It occurred to me that with my family history and professional background, I could develop a message that would help educate a broader audience about how to avoid many of the money problems that were occurring. In a way, I saw that helping others overcome the obstacles to communication and successful transitions was a way in which I could give back to a larger community.

I began to apply what I had learned from my research to my client base. Each client was required to meet with me once a year to discuss any and all financial issues in addition to his investments. At those meetings, I began to ask the hard questions regarding the clients' transition plans and what they had done to prepare for these transitions and prepare their heirs. I began to consciously help facilitate the communication among family members concerning money issues that were arising or would arise. While many clients were resistant at first, over time, the lines of communication began to open up.

As I assembled my research and my thoughts on the subject, I started to give talks locally and in venues around the country. I became a guest speaker at Canyon Ranch resorts in 2005, talking about the real issues in transferring monies that high-net-worth families and their heirs face. I gave weekend interactive seminars on how to successfully communicate with family members about money during transition points. The response was enthusiastic, and the audiences seemed hungry for information on how to deal with the issues.

The process of reading, researching, and presenting led me to realize that all transition points, not just preparing for death, require money conversations if they are to be successful: divorce, remarriage and combining families, retirement, and dealing with aging parents. I began studying all of these transition points and the necessary ingredients for successfully discussing them and moving through them.

In November 2008, I launched a radio show, *The M Word*, that dealt with the topic of money issues and the necessary conversations around money during difficult economic times, like the one that we were in the midst of at that time, and at different stages in life. For three years, my guests and I explored all the various transition points in life and discussed why it is so difficult to have the money conversations, what the basic issues related to each transition stage in life are, and how we can have the critical conversations around these issues. My goal for this book is to address these topics in even greater depth and provide for the reader a framework for having successful Money Talks through all life's transitions.

I have learned there are many reasons why families do not communicate about money. There are the basic elements of control, trust, and family members' level of knowledge. But there are also less obvious factors, such as gender, age, cultural/social issues, anthropological/instinctual issues, psychological issues, and even neurological issues that need to be addressed or overcome. This book explores all these factors, helps you understand them, and provides a set of guidelines and steps to follow to overcome them.

Understanding why it is difficult to talk about family finances and learning how to have that conversation may or may not lead you to have the Money Talk. In the final analysis, you need to take that step on your own, perhaps with the help of your own advisors. For my family, understanding the reasons why Money Talks are so difficult, and continuing to have them over the years, has changed our money conversations and contributed to a healthier family life.

I have a wonderful husband of more than 30 years and two amazing sons. Together, my husband and I have taken the lessons I have read, studied, and learned by trial and error and from my radio show guests and the tools I have developed, and we have applied them to our family. We have raised two financially healthy sons. Money has *never* been a taboo subject in our household. My husband and I have always discussed financial matters with our children, beginning from age 10 onward. Like most parents of similar means, my husband and I set up investment accounts and 529 plans for our sons fairly early on. But unlike many families, we explained each account to our sons: what it was for, how much we had contributed, and when they would be able to access the money. I have even encouraged them to be savvy in their spending of the funds, as the monies remaining will eventually be theirs to invest in a home, business, or future educational endeavor.

Once the boys hit middle school, we started giving them weekly allowances. This exercise gave us the opportunity to discuss budgeting, saving, and philanthropy. But, I think just as important, the boys have witnessed firsthand our family money dimensions—how we acquire, use, and manage money—and our money values as we have tried to create a healthy balance among saving, spending, and giving. We have been consistently charitable in the community in which we reside based on our particular financial abilities. We established an endowment fund at our local Jewish Community Center in memory of my father and involved the boys in the recognition of the gift. We also encouraged them to be generous to local charities that they were interested in, and they have made us proud by giving donations through the years on their own with the monies they have earned. We bought life insurance policies for each son early on as a means of providing them with a slice of financial security and long-term protection.

Though my sons went to camp during their summer breaks, they did work part-time during their high school years. One worked at the local hospital sitting with elderly patients as part of a special program. The other started a small business with a friend, providing snow-removal services to neighbors. There is a school of thought that says that if you give kids money, it creates a disincentive for them to work hard in life. I disagree. I believe that if you talk about money in a productive way; use, manage, and structure it in healthy ways; and provide solid role models who transmit healthy values concerning money and work, children will learn that hard work creates meaning in life, and that money is a valuable tool if it is used wisely.

My two sons have accepted the roles they may play in the future as cotrustees and executors. They know that my husband and I have life insurance in trust and long-term-care insurance, and they know where all the documents are stored. We answer any questions they have, and we have continued to keep the lines of communication about all financial matters open. Money Talks are not dreaded events in our family. In fact, I am really looking forward to having Money Talks dealing with some future transitions, like our sons getting married or having children. And I am realistic enough to understand that some of these future conversations may also present new challenges.

1

The Money Talk

Why It Is So Hard to Talk About Money and Why It Is So Important

We confess everything else in our society—sex, crime, illness.
But no one wants to reveal what they earn or how they got it.
—Barbara Ehrenreich

Joe Stanford did not see it coming.

A successful and passionate litigator whose ramrod-straight 5-foot, 8-inch frame and steely blue eyes belied his almost 80 years, Joe was convinced that he would die before his wife, Beth. They met just after World War II at a community dance in Brooklyn, New York. When Joe saw the petite, raven-haired Beth, it was love at first sight. That was the beginning of a love affair that lasted more than 50 years. They married while Joe was in law school and started their family as soon as he graduated. Beth and Joe had four children in eight years, two boys and two girls, and raised them in an affluent New Jersey suburb. The family was the center of their life together. In 2004, Beth died suddenly of a heart attack at age 76. She left all her assets to Joe. Struggling to cope on his own, lost without Beth, and battling a slow-growing lung cancer, Joe passed away two years later, just after he turned 80.

Joe and Beth's four children were not on good terms with one another. The two boys had been close as children, but once the older of the two departed for college, they did not see each other much. Over the years, sibling rivalry and their parents' tendency to favor one child over the others at various times interfered with the children's ability to maintain close ties. Not coincidentally, they settled in different parts of the country: Atlanta, Chicago, Tucson, and another New Jersey suburb.

To add to the family tensions, Joe was a disciplinarian who did not communicate well with his kids. Beth, a housewife who deferred to her beloved spouse regardless of the issue, was reserved and unable to counteract or compensate for the cumulative effect of Joe's strictness and detachment, which had created years of ill will between parents and children.

The eldest child, Mitchell, had not spoken to either parent for years. He had been rebellious as a child, and his relationship with his parents had never fully healed. Joe and Beth both deliberately left Mitchell out of their wills.

In addition, Joe's will made provisions for the inheritance of the next oldest child, Carol, to skip her and go directly to her three children, on whom Joe doted. Both Mitchell and Carol were enraged about the "unfair treatment" of the different siblings, and their anger became a source of major family conflict. Mitchell and Carol contested Joe and Beth's estates.[1] The matter ended up being in the courts for years, with the result that the assets were depleted by more than a third because of legal fees, the changing of the guard in attorneys and trustees, and the lack of preparedness and investment knowledge of the adult children.

Worse than the financial results were the emotional damages. The four adult siblings still do not speak to one another. As a result of the complex alliances and animosities, the extended family's set of nine cousins, who were friends and saw one another regularly when they were growing up, now have little to do with one another. The family bonds were torn by the inequality of the distributions, by the silent anger that lay behind the unequal treatment, and by the family's collective inability to communicate effectively with one another.

Let's look at another situation with a much happier ending.

Sherry, a curvaceous and bubbly 5-foot-4-inch blonde, came from a midwestern farm family. While in college on the West Coast, she met and married Mike, a stocky, easygoing football player whose family had cofounded and taken public a major manufacturing business in California. After graduating, they remained in northern California. Mike went to work for the company, and Sherry stayed home to raise their three children. Tragically, Sherry died at the age of 49 after a brief battle with ovarian cancer. She left her estate in equal shares to Mike and their three children, Hannah, Samantha, and Will.

Mike eventually remarried a wonderful woman, Frances, who had been the office manager for Sherry's oncologist and became a family friend. Frances was respectful of her stepchildren, and they grew to adore her. That added to the tragedy when Frances's life was cut short by breast cancer after 15 years of marriage, leaving Mike a widower for the second time.

Over the years, Mike served as a superlative model for his children in terms of communicating about and using money. He was charitable and fair-minded, devoted to his church and to the employees of his family's company. All too familiar with mortality, Mike took steps to prepare his children to ultimately inherit his estate. He held regular annual meetings in which he was very clear with his children, both collectively and individually, about the composition of his estate. At first the kids laughed at how seriously Mike took these family board meetings, but over time they grew to appreciate them. Mike made sure that the children also knew all of his financial, business, and legal advisors, as well as the officers at the institutions where the family wealth was invested and managed. His children all grew up to become productive, hardworking, and community leaders. He set up educational trusts[2] for his six grandchildren, to which he regularly made gifts, and he created a charitable lead trust[3] before his death. He encouraged positive and open communication among his children about the family wealth. After Frances's death, Mike obtained approval from Samantha and Hannah to appoint their brother Will, an accountant who was the most knowledgeable about finances, to be the coexecutor[4] along with the bank.

Mike passed away at the age of 84. His estate was successfully probated[5] with no family or legal interference. He had assembled an exceptionally talented team of professionals to help with the process: an estate lawyer, an accountant, a banker, and a financial advisor. The executors submitted the will to the probate court in a timely fashion, the estate taxes and fees were paid, and the assets were distributed a year later as Mike had planned.

Not coincidentally, Samantha, Hannah, and Will continue to communicate with one another about issues that arise between them and within their families. They also handle their financial affairs with intelligence and forethought, and even act as trustees and guardians for one another with respect to their own estate plans.[6] They have been able to continue the same pattern of open communication and sound financial decision making that their parents had established.

What are the lessons from these two stories? Smooth family transfers of wealth aren't automatic, but they can take place. Unfortunately, they're quite rare.

There is a 70 percent failure rate in transferring wealth, that is, a loss of control of assets through mismanagement, poor investments, or the like, according to Roy Williams and Vic Preisser, authors of *Preparing Heirs: Five Steps to Successful Transition of Family Wealth and Values* and earlier studies by the Massachusetts Institute of Technology and *The Economist*. Williams and Preisser cite three reasons for the failure of these wealth transfers:

- Tax considerations, legal issues, and the absence of planning account for 15 percent of failed transfers.
- Inadequately prepared heirs account for 25 percent of failed transfers.
- Breakdowns in communication and trust within family units account for 60 percent of failed transfers.

What struck me when I first read these three reasons was that the first two could be mitigated or solved by addressing the third. Breakdowns in communication and trust are clearly at the heart of these failed transfers and the resulting losses.

Most families find the following phrases all too familiar: "I'd rather not talk about it"; "That isn't something we discuss"; or "We'll set up a time to chat about it later." Or they may simply refuse to respond to any requests for conversation and change the subject.

The "it" in these phrases is, of course, money. In far too many families, money is a dirty word, a taboo subject—the M Word. Talking about it can be disturbing and can cause enormous anxiety and conflict. Regardless of the amount or the source of the family's money, the number or the age of family members, or the family's economic or social status, it is difficult for most families to talk about money.

It is no surprise that most families often react to major life events—a birth, illness, death, or divorce—by making quick financial decisions at the time of these important transitions, rather than proactively and carefully evaluating all their options before the events take place. The same questions, regardless of the event, always arise: "Who is in charge?" "Whom can I talk to?" "Whom can I trust?"

I have found that the lack of trust and honesty about money in a relationship can often mirror a lack of honesty about other issues as well and can signal the presence of fear of discussing the subject.

Spouses often aren't honest with each other about how much the new spring clothing, summer vacation abroad, or recent piece of electronic equipment cost, or about their true financial health before and during marriage.

Elderly parents often refuse to discuss the issue of inheritance or their deteriorating health with their grown children. Who wants to think about death or loss of control? Parents who aren't elderly are worried about job security, business uncertainty, or changes in financial circumstances, and they keep quiet about their finances so as not to alert their kids, whether adolescents or adults.

Siblings often become estranged because of the terms of their parents' wills or their lack of a will, over the disparity in the economic distributions thus far, or over unequal burdens of taking care of mom or dad's daily living and financial needs, whether because of geography or because of competence.

All of these life events and the conflicts that ensue demonstrate that money is a difficult topic. In my experience, that's true of less dramatic events as well: the state of your personal finances; the status of the collective finances of family members in combined family situations, investment strategies, allowances for kids, the family budget and cash flow, college funding, insurance needs, health issues involving family members, retirement and estate planning, the role of financial advisors, and the preparation of heirs and family philanthropy. At some point decisions have to be made and actions have to take place to manage the various components of a financial plan. But all too often these decisions and actions are put off and not addressed until something happens: there is a death in the family, a divorce is contemplated, or a family member's health is in question. By then it is often too late for a dispassionate and carefully crafted conversation to take place.

The inability to communicate about important family matters is so common that it is often an element in popular culture. "Meet the Woggels," a 2012 episode of the award-winning series *30 Rock*, used the fear of communication as a plot device. Head writer Liz Lemon, played by Tina Fey, desperately tries to get network executive Jack Donaghy, played by Alec Baldwin, and his demanding, overbearing mother, Colleen Donaghy, played by Elaine Stritch, to tell each other how they feel after years of not communicating, since Colleen is critically ill. In the final scene, the mother and son finally quickly share extraordinarily intimate feelings with as much emotion as they would bring to discussing the weather, then instantly return to their traditionally uncommunicative selves.

While it can make for great comedic fodder, in real life, the inability to talk about money can have tragic results. But that need not be the case. The goal of *The M Word* is to show that, beyond the experience of the death of a loved one and the deep sadness and sense of loss that can be associated with a divorce or diminished capacity, life transitions that involve money can, in fact, yield positive "happy endings" if communication and trust are part of the family culture. Healthy family financial dynamics require members of the family to treat one another with respect and with some form of equality. They require members of the family to be appropriately informed and engaged in communication with one another about the family, its assets, and the issues surrounding the transition points. Trust has to exist, and communication needs to take place over an extended period of time. And the family leader needs to practice intelligent financial planning, usually with the help of competent and caring professionals.

Achieving this kind of healthy family financial culture is not easy. Family members need to work hard and sometimes reveal vulnerabilities and take emotional risks. There will be times when pushing forward and having the Money Talk will be difficult, maybe even painful.

But not having the talk can be disastrous to the well-being of our society's most important social structure: the family. The absence of this conversation places the family and its assets at risk. Like Joe and Beth, many families have their assets depleted and their members divided and separated for more than one generation. Saying nothing or saying the wrong things can cause real and potential rifts, both today and for years to come.

Adding to the urgency of this issue is that an unprecedented transfer of wealth is taking place in our country. According to the Center on Wealth and Philanthropy at Boston College, $15 trillion will be passing between 2007 and 2026, and more than $59 trillion will be passing between 2007 and 2061. Those in the greatest generation, those who fought in World War II, are passing their assets to their heirs, the baby boomers. And the boomers are now preparing to transfer their assets to their own children. There are big dollars involved, and the impact on families across the country is enormous and also unprecedented.

With a 70 percent failure rate when it comes to transferring wealth, in the context of this huge transfer of wealth that is taking place, large inheritances are being forfeited to lawyers, assets are being mismanaged, and relationships are being poisoned. I believe this is primarily because parents and children, husbands and wives, and brothers and sisters find it difficult, if not impossible, to talk to and trust one another when it comes to the family's money.

The bottom line is: if families do not talk about money, they can potentially lose both their money and their family.

So why is it so hard for families to talk about money? Why is it as hard to talk about money as it is to talk about sex? Why do relatives find discussing money matters such an embarrassing, sensitive topic? Why don't these necessary conversations take place regularly?

Advocates of a return to traditional family values and structures often argue that the shift in the composition of the American family is at the root of many of our problems.

There's no question that the family is the most basic unit for the preservation and transfer of wealth, both within the immediate family itself and from one generation to another. Just about every key life event in a family unit involves money: marriage, birth, divorce, remarriage and blending families, educating your children, dealing with health issues, caring for an elderly parent with long-term care issues, dealing with the transition of a family business, a new job or the loss of a job, a sudden financial reversal, retirement, and death.

And there's no question that today's economic unit, or household, is very different from what we would have thought of even 20 years ago. Dr. William H. Frey, an internationally known demographer, professor of population studies at the University of Michigan, and a senior fellow at the Brookings Institution, notes that the baby boomers led the trend away from traditional family units, marrying later or not at all and divorcing at high rates.

According to the U.S. Census Bureau, in 2011, the United States had 118,682,000 households, of which only 49 percent included a married couple. Compare that to 1960, when a robust 74 percent of households included a married couple. There is also a rising trend toward single moms and dads as the heads of households. Single moms made up nearly 11 percent of family households, while single dads made up nearly 3 percent.

Living arrangements in America are also rapidly changing, especially when it comes to both same-sex-couple households and the recognition of same-sex marriages by individual states.

Approximately 593,000 same-sex-couple households lived in the United States in 2010, or about 1 percent of all couple households, according to the American Community Survey conducted by the Census Bureau. But changing living arrangements do not appear to be a major factor making Money Talks more difficult. According to Williams and Preisser, the statistics on transferring assets between generations is not linked to family structure and extends beyond the United States. So if it is not the changing family composition that makes the Money Talk difficult, what does?

To answer that question, I asked nearly every guest who appeared on my radio show why he thought money is so difficult to discuss. I also read many enlightening books on this topic of communication from well-known experts such as Deborah Tannen, author of *I Only Say This Because I Love You* and *You Just Don't Understand: Men and Women in Conversation*, and Kerry Patterson, Joseph Grenny, Ron McMillan, and Al Switzler, authors of *Crucial Conversations: Tools for Talking when the Stakes Are High*. I studied books such as *Silver Spoon Kids*, by Eileen and Jon Gallo, and *Money Doesn't Grow on Trees: A Parent's Guide to Raising Financially Responsible Children*, by Neale S. Godfrey, which focus specifically on talking to your children about money.

As I did my research, one thing that struck me was that these books and others like them tend to touch only lightly upon the topic of having difficult financial conversations. Some of them avoided the M Word altogether and discussed every other issue that arose in a family or workplace. The few communication books that addressed the issue explored "money conversations" like asking your boss for a raise, discussing allowances, or speaking with siblings about the financial arrangements required to care for an aging parent. Aside from these few situations, most of the books about the communication breakdown between family members or others had little to say about money. And even if they did discuss the subject, there was no specific advice on *how* to engage in tough money conversations with family members.

Even Williams and Preisser, whose *Preparing Heirs* I found very insightful, focused mostly on generational wealth transition. Their book did not move beyond the generational transition issues to address all the other life transitions—marriage and divorce, for example—each of which has significant financial underpinnings. Nor did their book address the factors that make the Money Talk difficult, or how to overcome them.

After years of looking for an answer, I finally realized that there is no single reason; there are many, and they exist on different levels.

First, there are universal issues that simmer just below the surface, like the control of assets, the roles that various family members play, trusting one another, different values concerning money, behaving responsibly, health issues, interactions with advisors and counselors, and preparing heirs. People may or may not be aware of these factors, but in either case they wreck havoc when they aren't aired and dealt with head on.

Then there is an even deeper level of factors that are interfering with people having the Money Talk, like anthropological, psychological, sociological, neurological, age, gender, temperament, and cultural issues. Few people understand or are even conscious of these hidden factors that influence family conversations and, ultimately, family wealth. That's probably why books on communication have largely tended to avoid the issue.

Only by understanding these two levels of obstacles, bringing the issues to light, and addressing them can you diffuse the tension, anxiety, and challenge of the Money Talk.

In subsequent chapters, we'll take a deeper look at these issues and how to overcome them, but let's briefly look at the hidden issues in order to see just how complex the topic can be.

In *The Genius of Instinct: Reclaim Mother Nature's Tools for Enhancing Your Health, Happiness, Family and Work*, Dr. Hendrie Weisinger, a clinical/organizational psychologist, writes that humans have been hardwired to see money as an object of threat and control, and that the conversation is difficult because it is tied to the sexual exchanges that were part of money transfers in primitive societies. As a result, we link money and sex as mediums of exchange. When we say that we do not want to talk about money, this is rooted in our sexual behavior—another topic that very few people are comfortable discussing. Universally, sex is considered private, and most people are embarrassed about discussing it. (Embarrassment has an evolutionary function. For example, if you are embarrassed or ashamed about something, you will avoid that particular behavior.) So from an evolutionary perspective, according to Weisinger, the difficulty in talking about money is rooted in the concept of sexual exchange because that is exactly what we have ultimately used money for over thousands of years.

Freudian analysts also see money as a symbol for another medium of exchange, but for them it's a stand-in for feces, not sex. Freudian theory focuses on the infant earning the love of her parents through toilet training, so it is feces that is our earliest means of exchange, which is eventually replaced by money. This gives new meaning to phrases like "flushing money down the toilet" or "filthy lucre."

Individual money personalities and family and cultural patterns contribute to making the Money Talk problematic. A money personality, as defined by Theodore Millon, a professor of psychiatry at Harvard and the University of Miami, is how we think and feel about money and what we do relative to it. Millon believes that every individual develops a unique relationship with money in three dimensions: acquisition, use, and management.

Money takes on certain meanings within families and cultures, making the Money Talk even more complex. For example, the distribution of money in many families is equated with familial love. That is one of the reasons why, when family patriarchs distribute estate monies unequally or disinherit family members, the psychological fallout can be so disturbing to the family unit and the individual family members.

Money is used as a control mechanism in families and cultures, and therefore, bringing up the topic can be off limits. Some cultures have superstitions around money—that talking about money will bring them bad luck. From the psychological perspective, money is tied up with our personal sense of self-esteem, self-worth, and even familial love.

Social and cultural mores that have been passed down through generations have created certain attitudes about money that often make it difficult to have the conversation. The British have always thought that it was "vulgar" to talk about money, and apparently our Founding Fathers brought this value with them when they landed on the shores of America. Perhaps this is where our society's economic elite learned to think that talking about money was impolite, a way of thinking that is still pervasive today.

Even language plays a factor in making the Money Talk difficult. Colloquial expressions like "stinking rich" or "wallowing in money" reflect a certain negative association. The act of not speaking about the subject might be tied to avoiding the "degradation" or "degeneracy" associated with the idea of "having it." Consider the origin of the word *money*. It comes from the word *moneta*, derived from the Latin word *moneo*, which means "warn" or "warning." Perhaps this might help explain the caution people have had around money since early times. In Roman mythology, Moneta was a name related to the Roman goddess Juno Moneta, the wife of Jupiter. One of her responsibilities was to warn the Romans of impending danger. In a tribute to her, the Romans built a temple in her honor on Capitoline Hill. It later became the place where money was coined and kept. The word *moneta* entered Old French as *moneie*, and eventually became our word *money*. *Moneta* came into Old English as *mynet*, which was transformed into the word *mint*, the place where money is coined.

The American national character contributes to our having a hard time talking about money. As a nation, we've always been conflicted about money: we strive for wealth and equality at the same time. The nineteenth-century French philosopher and historian Alexis de Tocqueville, discussing Americans' attitudes toward money in *Democracy in America*, wrote: "I know of no other country where love of money has such a grip on men's hearts or where stronger scorn is expressed for the theory of permanent equality of property." The downside of democracy, he argued, is an excessive drive for individualism and materialism.

We can even look at a relatively new area called neuroeconomics to search for reasons why it is difficult to talk about money.

As I develop further in Chapter 3, a knowledge of basic neurological engineering can help individuals understand the role the brain plays in the economic decisions we make every day, according to *Your Money and Your Brain: How the New Science of Neuroeconomics Can Help Make You Rich,* by Jason Zweig, a *Wall Street Journal* columnist.

Another contributing factor is gender differences. These are huge when it comes to personal communication, money values, and risk tolerances. Women typically focus on long-term rather than short-term gains and have a greater commitment to planning around their children and life events. These differences between men and women can largely be explained by neurological differences in the brain. Studies involving more than a million participants worldwide have confirmed these differences, showing that they are consistent regardless of place or origin or language, according to Barbara Annis, a leading expert in leadership and gender initiatives and author of *Leadership and the Sexes: Using Gender Science to Create Success in Business.*

Marriage politics is also a factor, especially in couples in which women equal or surpass their spouses in both education and earning power. At the beginning of the national economic downturn, the gender reversal trend was reinforced in part because the recession hurt the employment of men (in predominantly male industries) more than that of women. Males accounted for about 75 percent of the 2008 decline in employment among prime working-age individuals, according to the U.S. Bureau of Labor Statistics.

Making the Money Talk even more difficult is that all these factors play out differently in every family and every situation. So not only are we dealing with a long list of targets, but they're constantly moving targets as well. Let's look at how this played out in two families.

Jake and Sara Green, a recently married couple, both of whom had been married previously, needed to zero in on the topics of trust and money values as they began their relationship. Jake and Sara came to their relationship with different sets of money values and experiences with trust that they had learned from their nuclear families and acted out in their first marriages. Neither of them brought children to their new relationship. Jake is a 43-year-old professor of economics at an Ivy League university. Sara is a 37-year-old professional musician, playing violin in a symphony orchestra.

Jake's father, Larry, was a gambler who was in and out of businesses throughout his life. As a result, the family went through repeated boom-bust financial cycles. Fortunately, Larry's last business venture was successful, and he was able to retire with a healthy nest egg. As a result of listening to his advisor, Larry was able to establish trusts for each of his three kids.

Jake understandably does not have a sense of financial security and does not trust those around him to fulfill their obligations or meet his financial needs. He lives with a fear of spending money and not having enough. These fears were perpetuated by his first marriage to a woman who was a risk taker and a compulsive spender.

Sara, on the other hand, had a more predictable upbringing. She had always felt secure about money and used and managed it wisely. Her father was a schoolteacher, and her mother worked as an office clerk at an insurance company. Sara was an only child, raised in a sober but not parsimonious middle-income household. Financial differences didn't play a major role in her divorce.

Jake had never actually articulated his thoughts and fears about money, but they were certainly in play when he and Sara decided to buy a house. They were house hunting in a bucolic community that was both near Jake's university and within commuting distance of the city where Sara's orchestra was located. Jake was convinced that they should pay for the house in cash. Sara, on the other hand, was comfortable taking on a small mortgage, with the understanding that the monies that were not used for the purchase of the house could be invested in a way that could potentially yield[7] a better return. That had worked for her parents, and she didn't see why it should not work for her and Jake.

Their advisor worked with Jake and Sara, facilitating their Money Talk and helping them come up with ways to bridge the differences between their money personalities and family cultures. They had each brought separate monies to the relationship, and they agreed to keep the bulk of those assets in separate accounts. They would make equal contributions toward the purchase of the house and toward a joint account equal to the balance of the mortgage. The house would be held jointly, with the mortgage in both names.

This suitable solution, which appears so simple and obvious on paper, was achieved only after they agreed to have the Money Talk and, through it, recognized their different money histories and values. The process brought them closer together. They recently called their advisor to help them with another Money Talk, this time about becoming parents.

Sam Miller is a strapping 6-foot 2-inch 58-year-old who participates in triathlons. For more than 20 years, he worked as an investment banker at a boutique firm on Wall Street. Sam was laid off during the financial crisis when a larger bank bought his firm and downsizing began. Because of his age and the changing nature of the financial world, Sam had trouble landing a similar well-paying job. The only work he'd been able to find was as manager of a large retail store in a mall near their home.

Sam's wife, Lorraine, cuts a striking figure. A former college basketball player who worked briefly as a fashion model, she looks like she could step back into either role today, despite being 56. A talented entrepreneur, Lorraine had launched a small gift basket shop and expanded it into a corporate promotions business. However, in light of the recession and the earning limitations of her industry, the combination of her income and new modest salary was insufficient to maintain their former lifestyle. Over the years, the Millers had become comfortable with spending lavishly on themselves, but also, more important, being generous in their gifting to their children.

As a result, their assets were being depleted steadily by expenditures that were greater than their salaries and withdrawals of monies from their investments that were greater than the returns generated by the portfolio. Sam and Lorraine found it difficult to talk about their situation. Sam, who was in charge of the family finances, could not bring himself to alert Lorraine to the unfortunate situation they were in.

When they finally came to speak with me, we discovered that the issue of control was paramount for Sam. He had to relinquish control over the family finances and the interactions with the family's financial advisor: me. Gender issues also played a role. Lorraine had to raise her awareness and knowledge level and take a more active role in working with me. There were other issues simmering below the surface as well. They were dealing with the social stigma associated with a change in financial circumstances and the loss of self-esteem that comes when you cannot maintain the same lifestyle as everyone else in your social circle.

As their advisor, I was able to help them work through these issues and have a series of important Money Talks. We drafted an agenda for each meeting and created a safe, secure, and interesting environment for the discussions. These Money Talks weren't miraculous. The Millers have had to make some hard choices and sacrifices. But their relationship and their family have remained strong, and by addressing their money issues, they've been able to stabilize their financial life.

I cannot sit down with each of you and facilitate your own family's Money Talk. This book is my effort to provide the same kind of advice, counsel, and help that I would give if we were sitting together in my office. To accomplish that, I have divided the process I have developed into five steps. Having read this chapter, you have already learned why the Money Talk is so important and why it is so hard.

The first step, and the subject of Chapter 2, is exploring what life transitions your family is facing and then determining the topics, issues, and conversations that need to take place as a result. I have already touched on the Money Talk issues that potentially surround estate transfers, remarriage, and financial setbacks, but there are many others. In Chapter 2, you will learn that every transition point in life is a money transition.

Take a young couple who are fresh out of graduate school and eager to marry. One or both of them may be saddled with school or family loans. They cannot find jobs in their fields that pay enough to cover their basic expenses if they were living on their own in an expensive urban center. They've moved in "temporarily" with one set of parents while they get a financial plan together and gather the resources to move out and begin their independent life together. What financial tools and communication skills do they need in order to have the right conversations, create an appropriate financial plan, and ultimately build a successful life together?

Think about the issues surrounding the aging of parents. This is even more dramatic when the parents suffer from dementia, Alzheimer's, or any other degenerative physical or mental condition. They forget to pay their bills, fall victim to unethical advisors, and sometimes do not even remember what day it is or where they are. How can adult children take over the management of their parents' financial affairs without taking away their parents' dignity or inciting deep-seated resentment? The actions may be part of an effort to make sure that the money is not misappropriated and that there will be enough money for the ailing parent or parents to live during their final years in the fashion that they require or have become accustomed to. The longer this painful Money Talk is put off, the greater the odds that the aging parents' physical and psychological conditions will continue to deteriorate and will unintentionally sabotage the entire process. The sooner the process is started, the easier it will be. How and when should you have the respectful and productive conversation about these issues, before your parents' resources are unnecessarily depleted and family discord creates irreparable damage to relationships? In Chapters 3 through 7, you will learn specifics about confronting five of the most significant and common life transitions.

In Chapter 8, you will take the next step: learning to recognize and understand all the factors that prevent us from having the Money Talk. These include both the universal factors (the control of assets, the roles that various family members play, trusting one another, different money values, behaving responsibly, health issues, interactions with advisors and counselors, and preparing heirs) and the deeper level of factors, such as anthropological, psychological, sociological, neurological, age, gender, temperament, family history, and cultural issues. Only by understanding these obstacles, learning how to bring them to light, and formulating ways to overcome them can you make the Money Talk a regular feature of your family's life.

Once you have removed the roadblocks, you can begin to think about how to conduct a successful Money Talk. That's the subject of Chapter 9. In it, you will learn how to prepare the agenda for your conversation and conduct successful conversations around difficult topics.

Our family and money lives are so complex that few of us can, or should, manage them without some professional help. In Chapter 10, you will learn how to select and work with professionals who will contribute to a healthy family financial dynamic. You want advisors who will support and help your efforts to have healthy communications about money.

Money Talks aren't one-time events. Depending on your circumstances, they could be annual or even weekly discussions. In Chapter 11, you will be reminded that a commitment to having repeated discussions about money issues is key to successfully tackling all the financial issues arising out of life's transitions: births, marriages, divorces, remarriages, blending families, changes in careers and financial circumstances, the return of adult children to the home, declining health status, transferring wealth, preparing heirs, and deaths.

My goal in this book is to demonstrate how families can start these discussions and keep them going to make certain that family assets are properly invested, maintained, and, when the time comes, fairly divested. I will show you how to turn the dinner table or other venues for conversation into a meaningful financial "summit meeting" for the entire family, with a low-key approach in which everyone voices and listens to all opinions, then the family forms a mutually workable financial blueprint. These guidelines are necessary now as never before, as many individuals and families, as a result of the recent Great Recession, are earning less, receiving less yield on their investments, and worrying about their financial security more than ever.

Despite today's circumstances and the inherent sadness that is sometimes involved, happy endings can occur in many kinds of life transitions that involve money, from marriage and divorce to the loss of a business or a job to end-of-life issues . . . as long as everyone in the family who is affected is informed to some degree, fully respected, and engaged in responsible communication about the family assets.

I have found that when money matters are approached with consideration, respect, and a degree of openness, everyone shares the emotional and financial rewards. Animosity and rancor can be avoided if families (immediate, extended, or single-parent; two-family mergers; or whatever type of family units you have created) sit down together and talk to one another—not just from the wallet, but from the heart.

Money is probably the most difficult subject for all of us to discuss. But by picking up this book and reading this first chapter, you have drawn back the curtain, acknowledged the elephant in the room, and exposed it to the light of day. It might not seem so right now, but you have actually already overcome the most difficult hurdle. Let's keep the momentum going by taking the first step in my five-step process: delving more deeply into life's transitions and determining where you are and what are the topics and issues you will need to address to be able to have a successful Money Talk.

Things to Think About

- When was the last time you started a conversation about money with your partner, spouse, sibling, child, or parent?
- Do you regularly have discussions about money with your family, or do you avoid the topic whenever you can?
- Do you find it easier to talk about sex than about money? Or do you find both subjects difficult to talk about?
- Did you have a good role model in life when it came to acquiring, using, and managing money? What about having money conversations?

(continued)

- If you had a good role model, who was it and what did you learn from her?
- If your role model was not optimal, what did you learn from him that you know you need to change?
- Were there times in the past when your family should have had a Money Talk but did not? How did things turn out?
- After reading about some of the reasons why it is difficult to talk about money, which issues resonated most with you? Why do you think those particular issues really hit home?
- Are you currently going through a transition stage in life, such as remarriage, retirement, or taking over the responsibility for an aging parent?
- If you are, have you discussed the issues you find challenging with your significant other or a family member that they relate to? For example, have you spoken with your spouse about your worries about your retirement lifestyle?
- Have you experienced any type of economic or financial loss in your life in the last 24 months that requires a Money Talk: loss of job, loss of spouse, or loss of investments?
- Have you expressed your fears and concerns about this loss to anyone?

2

Life's Transitions

Where Are You in Life, What Issues Are You Facing, and Which Money Conversations Need to Take Place?

The only sense that is common in the long run is the sense of change—and we all instinctively avoid it.
—E. B. White

Every transition point in life is a money transition. You might think, "Of course you see the world through a financial lens; you are a financial advisor." But if you dig beneath the surface, no matter what life change or stage you are experiencing, you will see that money is involved and is a key component driving it. Are you looking for a new job or business? Are you going through a painful divorce? Are you evaluating long-term-care options for either your parents or yourself? Are you considering a plan to retire in the next five years or a revision to your estate plan given your current circumstances? In the back of your mind, or maybe at the very front, it is likely that you are assessing the financial impact of your options.

Take a look at this list of transitions and the personal finance issues that each may raise.

- If you are getting married, you should disclose your assets, liabilities, and goals; decide whether to merge or segregate your individual finances; and discuss any lifestyle compromises that may be necessary.

- When you are starting a family, it is vital to figure out how you will provide your children with short-term and long-term financial security and education funds.
- Getting divorced means having to divide marital assets while trying to preserve financial stability and family sanity.
- Remarriage often involves the blending of disparate family cultures and lifestyles, and deciding on individual and joint responsibilities and obligations.
- Changing your job or shifting careers typically mandates a fresh self-assessment of your skills and your value in the open market, an updated look at your current finances, and possibly a reevaluation of your goals.
- Experiencing a decline in financial circumstances forces you to recalculate your cash flow, reassess your lifestyle, and settle on new spending and gifting patterns.
- If you or a family member is diagnosed with a serious illness requiring long-term care, you will need to assess the current and expected costs, determine your existing income resources, and integrate insurance and other instruments that can help support the necessary care.
- Having to take over the affairs of an aging parent means determining the person's financial health, then developing estate planning and healthcare strategies that will provide both asset protection[1] and quality care.
- "Boomerang kids" returning to the nest should prompt a calculation of the effect of the return on individual and family finances, and the drafting of a plan to maintain family harmony, parental assets, and the adult child's financial and emotional independence.
- Preparing for retirement today means reevaluating portfolios and expectations based on new economic circumstances and increased longevity.
- A death in the family forces family members to assess the financial effect on their own lives and should lead to the proper

distribution of estate assets, the payment of required taxes, and the eventual settling of the estate.

- If you are going to prepare your heirs and plan for a successful estate transfer,[2] you will need to transfer family values and also provide meaningful education and any necessary professional support.
- Transferring a family business requires creating a plan that addresses some very complex, multigenerational financial and psychological issues involving the dynamics and health of both the family and the business.

Individual family members are constantly moving from one life phase to the next. It is rare that any two family members are experiencing the same transition at the same time. Perhaps you are getting ready for your late in life second child, one of your siblings is getting remarried, another has just graduated with a master's degree and returned home in preparation for launching a new career, and your parents are feverishly planning for their retirement and caring for an ailing elderly relative. Money issues are prevalent in each of these stressful changes. It is important to understand that the financial issues differ depending on the transition. However, just being aware that each family member is going through a different stage of life with its own unique issues is not enough. You need to determine where you are and where the other family members are, and to understand all the topics and issues you will need to address if you are to have a successful Money Talk.

Unfortunately, given the number of transition points and their various complexities, I cannot cover all of them in this book. Instead, I have chosen a few that I think will resonate with most readers today: changes in financial circumstances, remarriage and merging families, retirement planning, aging parents and long-term-care needs, and preparing heirs and transferring assets, including a closely held family business.

If you are in the midst of, or shortly about to face, one of these transitions, I am sure you will turn directly to the chapter that addresses your immediate concern. That is not just natural;

it is wise. However, once you have read the chapter you believe is most important to you at this moment, please take the time to go back and read the others as well. It is never too early to prepare for future transitions. And if you have already gone through one of the transitions, understanding why things may have transpired the way they did can provide insight into your future Money Talks. It could also help you prepare the rest of your family for facing the transition themselves.

Things to Think About

- What stage are you at in your own life?
- What transition point(s) are you going to face in the short-term, the medium-term, and the long-term future?
- Do you have any plans in place, even in just a rudimentary state, to deal with these upcoming life events?
- What issues are you confronting with your short-term transition?
- Have you spoken with any family members about these issues?
- If you have spoken with them, have the conversations gone well? Have they been productive and helpful, or have they been painful and detrimental?
- If you have not spoken with anyone, why is that? Are others unwilling to have the conversation, or are you?
- Do you think including advisors in these conversations might help? What kind of advisors do you think would be best suited to the role?
- Other than helping to orchestrate conversations, what other tasks could your advisors perform?
- Do you have a structure or plan in place to deal with the transition you are facing?

(continued)

- If not, whom can you work with to help you create one?
- If you do have a plan in place, does it need to be revised?
- Are your family members and advisors all aware of the plan, and have they had a chance to comment on it?
- Have you had a meeting to discuss the finalized plan and make sure everyone is on board with it?
- What documents and instruments might you need in order to execute your plan of action?
- If you have those documents and instruments already in place, which ones may need to be revised?

3

Changes in Financial Circumstances

Having Money Talks when Disaster Strikes—or when Good Fortune Comes Your Way

*I'm living so far beyond my income that we may
almost be said to be living apart.*
—e. e. cummings

It is always helpful to add a little humor to a serious situation, but pithy quotes aside, significant changes in a family member's financial circumstances or a situation in which income and expenses have not been properly aligned is a serious matter. As we slowly come out of the Great Recession, the worst economic downturn since the Great Depression, economists and pundits are just now assessing the destructive impact of this tumultuous financial maelstrom on Americans.

More jobs were lost in the recession between 2007 and 2009 than in the previous four recessions combined. As in the previous three recessions, less educated workers were more vulnerable to layoffs than more educated employees. But even those with college degrees saw their vulnerability to layoffs increase over time, according to an analysis by Henry S. Farber of the Bureau of Labor Statistics Displaced Workers Surveys. In his 2011 paper titled *Job Loss in the Great Recession: Historical Perspective from the Displaced Workers Survey, 1984–2010*, he wrote that the job loss rate of those with college degrees during 2007 through 2009 was 11 percent. That is the highest level observed since the Displaced Workers Survey data were first collected in the early 1980s. There are business owners who have had to stop operations as a result of competition from overseas, and highly educated professionals have lost their jobs in the wake of the economic contraction and corporate consolidations that have occurred. Even those who have not lost their business or their job have been affected by the declines in real estate, construction, finance, and manufacturing.

As of the writing of this book, we are in the midst of a recovery, albeit a slow and selective one. The economy lost 8.8 million total jobs during the downturn, and, despite the creation of several million new private-sector jobs, it will take time to create enough jobs to both replace those lost and provide new ones for the next generation of workers. Some sectors are coming back, but others are not. And with large numbers of young people steadily entering the job market, and even larger numbers of preretirees still unemployed, many families will continue to face changes in their financial circumstances for years to come.

The subject of money is difficult for families to discuss under normal circumstances. Given today's economic and personal financial challenges, the topic is even more emotionally charged, and the need for the Money Talk is even greater. Many parents are understandably nervous about the fate of their fortunes over the long term and about the financial futures of their children. In turn, these children are anxious as a result of their parents' fears and their own reduced employment opportunities. The natural instinct in such circumstances is for everyone to shut down emotionally and avoid the conversation. But doing so can be costly—and not just in dollars and cents. Putting off a Money Talk can lead to the emergence of all kinds of emotions and family conflicts, such as sibling rivalry, marital anxiety, and uneasy questions of control, making the need even greater. These emotions and conflicts, in turn, can stir up more fears, which lead to further family anxiety. Soon you have a cyclical downward spiral in which the aversion to addressing the initial financial conversation causes more financial difficulties, making the conversation even harder psychologically.

Because of the sheer magnitude of the number of people affected, it is no surprise that the impact of these economic challenges has made its way into pop culture. In the 2011 motion picture *The Company Man*, Ben Affleck plays an affluent marketing executive who loses his job in the transportation industry. He painfully displays the chain of emotions and behaviors that result as he desperately tries to deal with the loss: disbelief, shame, anger, denial, and an inability to openly and honestly discuss the major financial calamity with his wife and family.

As with any serious problem, you cannot deal with change if you do not acknowledge it. It is absolutely necessary that you disclose the changes in your financial circumstances to your family members and discuss these changes with them so that the necessary steps can be taken to adjust, and an action plan for managing the family's financial assets intelligently can be implemented. In wealthier families, for example, the monthly provision of living expenses for certain family members and the annual gifting of assets to children may have to be reduced to preserve enough assets for the parents' expected life expectancies. Family members have to work together to maintain the personal dignity of each individual and the health of the family unit.

Unfortunately, not every family deals with the situation well. There are many people who continue to spend and go further into debt because they are ashamed to discuss the change in their financial circumstances with the members of their family. The stories about terminated individuals hiding their new situation are not apocryphal. I recently heard about an individual who had lost his job and refused to tell his spouse or his family. Rather than confront this difficult situation head on and deal with his feelings of embarrassment, shame, and personal disappointment, he took on odd jobs and pretended to be going to his old job, even when he had nowhere to go. Luckily, Amy and Trevor Dorset did not follow that pattern.

Amy, who is a dynamic and effusive 54-year-old, worked as a senior human resources executive at a publicly traded financial services firm. As part of a restructuring and consolidation after a merger, she was laid off. Her husband, Trevor, is a quiet, curly-haired 56-year-old real estate attorney whose previously successful private practice had been struggling through the recession.

The Dorsets had huge monthly expenses to cover. They had recently built a four-bedroom vacation home on the beach in Nags Head, North Carolina, with the hope of retiring there in the future. Their full-time home was a beautiful, spacious suburban Boston colonial with more than an acre of land. They also maintained an apartment in Boston for their 26-year-old daughter, Jillian, who was attending a public policy graduate school program at Harvard.

Because of the industrywide consolidations that were taking place, Amy's prospects of finding a similar high-paying senior human resources position were not good. The Dorsets realized that they might have to consider selling one of their homes and changing their lifestyle in some ways. Amy had stock options, but many of them were under water. It would take time to realize value from them, and now was not the right time to sell.[1] The Dorsets's 22-year-old son, Jonathan, was living at home while interviewing for jobs after graduating from college. The couple also oversaw the care for Amy's mother, who was in a local assisted-living facility.

The Dorsets had a lot on their plate. It was time to talk. They needed to have a series of conversations with each other and with their children to discuss the necessary lifestyle and financial changes. Amy and Trevor first examined their finances. Like many busy professionals, they had not comprehensively examined their money situation for years. Amy had always deferred to her husband on financial matters. But given his crazy work schedule as a sole proprietor and her constant business travel, they were not always able to communicate and plan ahead.

The couple called a meeting with their financial advisor—who had been suggesting a thoughtful discussion with their accountant and their attorney—to work through all the elements of their finances and come up with a plan. It was also a good chance for Amy and Trevor to get on the same page with regard to the family finances. The Dorsets also called a family meeting with Jillian and Jonathan. Together, Amy and Trevor identified and communicated the stresses they were feeling as well as some of the changes the family would need to make.

The Dorsets had significant amounts of debt that they wanted to restructure.[2] They agreed to pay down some of the debt while refinancing all the properties at lower rates. To provide some ready cash, Amy began to sell the company stock she had acquired, and she agreed to start a program of selling awards as they vested and as soon as it made sense. With the sudden time off, Amy had an opportunity to think about other areas in their life where they could improve and simplify. They considered renting their new vacation home, and they looked for a less expensive rental for their daughter in Boston. The couple even considered selling their large and expensive-to-maintain colonial and buying a more reasonably priced empty-nest abode. Although Amy and Trevor were rational and sensible people, surrounding themselves with reasonable advisors who could help them with these difficult conversations and decisions was key to assembling the final plan and making sure it was properly executed. After an in-depth assessment of their finances, it was clear they could make the necessary changes without significantly altering their lifestyle. Unfortunately, not every family is that lucky.

Alan Hopper, an imposing 62-year-old British expatriate with a gregarious manner, was a high-earning compliance officer at a financial services company. Business had not been the same since the big 2008 meltdown and the fall of Lehman Brothers. When his firm decided to trim the budget and eliminate some senior positions, Alan was asked to take a new job and a 30 percent pay cut. His wife, Doreen, a slightly overweight, well-dressed woman, did not take an interest in the family finances. Each year, she blindly signed her name to a joint tax return that was filled with large charitable contributions to the Red Cross, the National Wildlife Federation, and other organizations, and also a sizable interest deduction for their mortgage.

Alan, a proud and somewhat old-fashioned man, has a difficult time talking about money. He was in denial about his pay cut. For many months he refused to speak to his wife about the change in his job or the need to alter the family spending patterns. As a result, they went further into debt. Alan started taking early withdrawals from his large IRA[3] without discussing the matter with his wife or other family members. It was not until the following year's tax return was filed that his accountant brought up the subject with Alan. His accountant highlighted the significant penalties from the IRA withdrawals and, despite the current low rates, the increasing interest expense outlay to carry the burgeoning debt. He thought it was time to help Alan come to terms with what was going on. The accountant, who had a good relationship with Doreen, was able to intercede and help facilitate the conversation between the spouses.

Once Doreen learned of their changed financial circumstances, she began to take a more active role in the family finances. She realized that her husband's negligent and irresponsible behavior was affecting the family's financial stability and their children's future. I have found that when family and children are at financial risk, previously uninterested women take a sudden interest in money matters. After much discussion, conflict, debate, and more than a little anger, Alan and Doreen were able to formulate a new game plan for their spending. They learned some important lessons in the process. They finally understood that they needed to openly and honestly share financial information with each other. Doreen learned that she could no longer defer to Alan on money matters. They also learned the importance of having a good, solid financial advisor on board to help them come to terms with the reality of their situation.

A change in the financial circumstances of any family member, not just one of the primary earners, can significantly impact the family and require a Money Talk. Take the case of Paul and Anne Zacharia and their son, Timothy.

Paul is a 62-year-old human resources executive with a media company. His wife, Anne, is a successful pediatric dentist. The Zacharias live in a lovely three-bedroom condominium in a suburb of Philadelphia. They sold their larger split-level home four years ago, when their son Timothy had graduated from college, found a good job with a technology start-up, and moved into a downtown apartment of his own.

The company that Timothy was working for was bought by a larger firm that was looking to acquire the start-up's applications and incorporate them into its own products. While Timothy received a nice settlement in the process, he soon afterward found himself out of work in a stagnant economy. After he had been unemployed for almost a year, the lease on his apartment came up for renewal. Understandably fearful about committing to another year, Timothy approached Paul and Anne and asked if he could move back home temporarily.

The Zacharias, despite being devoted to their son and willing to do whatever they could to help him, knew that his moving back home might become a challenge. Fortunately, they decided to have a Money Talk and address the issues involved. The Zacharias decided to draft a "contract" that, once fully "executed," was prominently displayed on the refrigerator. Timothy agreed to clean his room once a week, to be involved in kitchen cleaning and cooking duty, and to be respectful of his family when entertaining his friends at the condo. Financially, Paul and Anne agreed to cover his food, his auto loan, and his out-of-pocket medical expenses and car insurance, while Timothy would cover his gas, his car maintenance, his cell phone, extra food, and entertainment.

As you might imagine, Timothy's return required an adjustment: he hadn't lived at home for more than eight years. But it worked. Whenever he had an issue with his parents or they had an issue with him, they were able to talk about it. Rather than an ordeal, Paul and Anne feel that it has been a valuable opportunity for them to revisit their relationship with their son and spend some quality time together. It gave them a chance to get to know their son on a new level based on mutual respect, and it helped them forge adult relationships.

After a little less than a year of living with his parents, Timothy landed a job with another software firm, this one located in New York. Anne has been surprised that the condo that she and Paul were afraid would feel confining with Timothy in residence now seems somewhat empty with his absence.

Changes in financial circumstances are not always negative. While in today's world, they are most often a function of the economic downturn or the loss of a job, they can also be for the better. After working hard for many years, you could find yourself living a lifestyle that is within your current means, and then overnight be confronted with a new and larger set of economic options and decisions. That is what happened to Larry Long.

Larry is a highly talented 44-year-old electrical engineer who competes in Ironman triathlons in his spare time. Larry worked for a Silicon Valley–based technology company from its inception in 1996. The founder had recruited him to head a specific project for the company.

Larry, his wife, Jane, and their three young sons lived in a very modest home outside San Francisco. When the company went public in 2005, they received a small fortune overnight. Larry was completely unprepared for what it meant for him and the family. Jane no longer had to work as a marketing manager. The boys now had new options for education at private schools. They could completely renovate their modest home, or they could move to a much larger and more luxurious home in a more affluent neighborhood.

The Longs were confronted with a number of issues they had never considered before. They had to examine their values, their attitudes toward money, how they wanted the newfound wealth to affect Jane's life and their children's lives, what lifestyle they wished to lead, and the need to structure their assets and their estate to reflect their new economic status. For the first time, the Longs were in need of a financial advisor, an accountant, and a lawyer who could advise them on the myriad of issues and decisions they would have to make. Their longtime tax advisor had experience only with clients filing simple tax returns. Even before their windfall, the Longs had been the most affluent of his clientele. The Longs realized that they needed to build a team of advisors who had experience counseling high-net-worth clients and would be able to help them with all the new decisions they would be required to make. They had not just outgrown their home; they had outgrown their advisor as well.

Changes in financial circumstances—for better or worse—require the courage and fortitude to address the situation head-on. The best time to discuss finances is as soon as you see the change approaching. If the change is sudden, with no advance notice, then the time to begin the conversation is as soon as possible. Job losses, sudden illnesses, and unexpected increases in wealth are all events that require an M Word conversation.

Things to Think About

- Discussing money is difficult during normal times. When family finances are under great stress the topic becomes even more important and emotionally charged.
- While the natural instinct to avoid the topic is even stronger in difficult financial times, the financial need to have the discussion is even greater.
- Difficult times can exacerbate emotions and family conflicts, increasing the anxiety and prompting delay, which leads to more financial harm, which leads to more anxiety and a terrible downward spiral.
- It is essential to disclose the true nature of the changes in financial circumstances to family members so everyone can understand the need for adjustments and contribute to the plan.

(continued)

- Remember that a change in the financial circumstances of any family member, not just the primary
  earner, can require a Money Talk.
- Improvements in financial circumstances also require
  a Money Talk so the family can successfully adapt to
  additional income or wealth.
- The best time to have Money Talks about changes in
  circumstances are as soon as the change becomes
  clear, or if it can't be foreseen, as soon as possible.

4

Remarriage and Merging Families

Having Money Talks when Divorcing and/or Getting Married Again

A divorce is like an amputation: you survive it, but there's less of you.
—Margaret Atwood

The statistics are well known, but still sobering. Nearly half of all marriages in the United States ended in divorce in 2009, according to "Number, Timing and Duration of Marriages and Divorces: 2009," from the Census Bureau's 2011 *Current Population Reports*. Less well known, and even more striking, is new research by Bowling Green State University sociologists Susan Brown and I-Fen Lin. In a paper titled "The Gray Divorce Revolution," they reported that the divorce rate of those 50 years old and older has doubled over the past 20 years. In 1990, one in ten divorces were of people 50 or older; by 2009, that number was one in four.

Most of us have been touched by divorce, whether in our own family or in our circle of friends. We have witnessed the emotional upheaval and sense of loss that families endure as part of the devastating emotional fallout. Despite that, many of those who get divorced end up remarrying. In 2008, 35 percent of recently married couples had at least one spouse who had been married before, according to Rose M. Kreider and Renee Ellis, authors of "Number, Timing and Duration of Marriages and Divorces: 2009." One would hope that couples would tend to get it right the second time around. However, with remarriage comes the merging of families, often with different characteristics, ages, economic circumstances, and money values. And, the statistics reflect the added conflicts. Second and subsequent marriages actually have a 150 percent greater chance of ending in divorce than first marriages. Indeed, 53 percent of the people over 50 who are now getting divorced have done so at least once before. In fact, if you are between 50 and 64 and have been married before, your risk of divorcing is actually doubled. The risk quadruples for those 65 and older.

Whether the remarriage is successful in the long term or not, the blending of families is difficult in both the short and the long term. While uniting later in life often means that couples have learned something from their previous mistakes, each individual is also likely to be more set in his ways. Individuals also often come with children, each of whom has unique characteristics and problems. Add the need to combine incompatible work and activity schedules and financial assets such as real estate, trusts, and personal holdings, and it is easy to understand the increased stress in a blended household.

And those are just the logistical issues. Remarriage, while certainly a joyous occasion, comes with an element that is not present in first marriages: loss. In remarriage, one of two life events, death and divorce, has affected at least one of the new marital partners. A sense of loss is endemic to all blended families, no matter how distant the divorce or the death. So initially, both partners need to recognize and work through that sense of loss. To be sure, marital transitions can be emotionally anguishing. It is in these situations that knowledge and communication are essential.

Those are two of the ingredients that made the marital transition of Julie Shine and Barry Greene so successful. After only 14 years of marriage, Julie, a 38-year-old schoolteacher with a dry sense of humor and a slight edge to her personality, had lost her husband. Marc, a computer programmer, had died of a massive heart attack at age 49. He left Julie financially comfortable while she raised their eight-year-old daughter, Ashley, alone. Four years later, Julie's best friend introduced her to Barry Greene, a handsome, fun-loving 44-year-old man who had lost his wife to lung cancer two years before. Barry's three kids, Alyssa, Allison, and Andrew, were 3, 5, and 7. Because Barry traveled a lot in his role as southeastern regional manager for a pharmaceutical company, he had hired a live-in housekeeper to care for his children. That all changed when Julie and Barry decided to get married.

While the love flowed easily between Julie and Barry, there was much work to be done between Ashley and her new siblings. As an only child, Ashley had had the sole attention of her mother for four years. By the time her mother got remarried, Ashley was a 13-year-old adolescent. For her part, Julie was not used to a house full of young children as well as an adolescent. Still, she did not want a live-in housekeeper, despite Barry's active travel schedule.

The dynamics were rocky for the first few years as each family member got to know the others. But it did not take long for the Greenes to become a well-adjusted family. What facilitated the process was the willingness and commitment of Julie and Barry to tackle the challenges they faced and seek outside support from professionals. They sought the help of a family therapist to help each child adjust to the new circumstances and to discuss important issues such as how discipline would be handled. Even before they got married, they went to a financial advisor to openly discuss their assets, their spending and saving habits, their financial goals, whether Julie would continue to work (she did), and who would pay for each child's summer camp, braces, and college.

While they did not think either of them had enough money to consider a prenuptial agreement, the first question they addressed was whether or not to blend their finances. It is not uncommon for very happily married couples with families to keep their finances separate, notes Jon Gallo, author of *Silver Spoon Kids*. In the Greenes' case, both were coming to the marriage with their own assets. While Julie was not a high earner, she did have a life insurance payout as well as an ongoing social security payout for her daughter. Barry had socked away a nice nest egg from working for Fortune 500 companies that offered various generous retirement plans. Despite this, Julie and Barry decided to pool their finances. They felt that their best years were ahead of them and believed that blending their finances would help promote unity within the family.

Dr. Gail Saltz, a psychiatrist and bestselling author, would say that Julie and Barry took the right action because they communicated honestly and planned accordingly at the beginning of their marriage. Saltz believes that money is a central theme in managing all the elements of a merged family: the individual temperaments and personalities, the family history and culture, the unique family structure, and the daily money maintenance. Saltz also believes that the money conversation has to be scheduled early on, and that full disclosure has to be its primary objective. She suggests that couples talk about what money means to them. Is it power? Is it security? I have found that the healthiest marriages are often based on up-front money disclosure. This demonstrates trust and confidence in the partner and the relationship early on. Providing disclosure and communicating the issues is not always easy, particularly when the individuals have histories of marriages that did not end well. Still, without open communication at the onset, the marriage could be fraught with conflict.

Unfortunately, not everyone is willing to open up—even to a marriage partner. No matter how intelligent, practical-minded, or successful in business a client might be, I have often found some who have a strong reluctance to confront the money realities and plan in advance during a first or subsequent marriage. Instead of having a level-headed conversation that is well planned and executed in an easy, matter-of-fact way, many couples let their emotions take over, refuse to address the necessary issues, and fail to put the right financial vehicles in place. Whatever the instruments or planning vehicles you use, they will not be as effective as they could or need to be without a financial plan that is acceptable to both parties.

While the Greenes did not need to consider asset protection, many couples enter relationships in which one has significantly more investments than the other. Talking about money is difficult as a matter of course. Bringing up the topic of a prenuptial agreement[1] as a means of protecting your assets can be frightening. From my client counseling experience, I have found that individuals may feel that it sets the wrong tone. At the beginning of a marriage a "what's mine is yours" sentiment is probably what they want to impart. They feel that broaching the subject of a prenuptial agreement could be seen as evidence of a "what's mine is mine" sentiment. That is the opposite of the message they want to give to their soon-to-be-spouse. In some cases, the partner who is asked to sign a prenuptial agreement views the request as indicative of a lack of trust within the relationship, even if the spouse requesting it only wants to be able to extricate the couple from the marriage if they find they have made a mistake.

One of my colleagues, a practicing estate attorney, told me about a client of his who was about to enter his third marriage. Before each marriage, the attorney had counseled his client to create a prenuptial agreement in order to provide protection for his heirs and his estate. The client refused each time. Before his third marriage, the client proudly exclaimed that after he tied the knot this time, he was staying in the marriage until he went to either the cemetery or the monastery.

Despite the unwillingness of some individuals to listen to advisors, entering or reentering marriage is exactly the kind of life event where a financial advisor, attorney, or accountant can help facilitate communication between the two partners. Often there needs to be a third person, a mutually acceptable party who understands the issues and has the trust of both spouses, to serve as an effective "mediator." Advisors can gently and wisely use the right words to help the soon-to-be-remarried couple gain insight concerning the benefit to both individuals. In many cases, a prenuptial agreement can actually take emotionally loaded financial topics off the table so that the couple can focus on building a life together.

In many prenuptial agreements, assets are kept separately in order to help protect them for children from a previous marriage or other designated heirs. In creating the prenuptial agreement, the financial and nonfinancial contributions of the spouse who has fewer assets are taken into consideration when resolving the disparity in wealth. It could be that the new wife has received a healthy monetary settlement from a previous marriage, but the new husband brings earning capability that has not been fully realized. The prenuptial agreement can be structured so that the spouse who brings less monetary wealth but a healthy cash flow is granted a yearly income, in the form of a distribution, that is added to her side of the balance sheet in the event of death or divorce.

For example, if you are a high-earning spouse, you may choose to pay a healthy sum of money annually to your partner, who may not have enough cash flow from separate assets to maintain his lifestyle, in order to satisfy the terms of the agreement. This money could be increased over time and other assets added, based on a schedule in the contract, should the marriage survive for certain designated time periods. Insurance policies could also be included as part of the agreement just in case a spouse dies prematurely.

The 2011 movie *New Beginnings*, in which actor Christopher Plummer loses his wife and, in his seventies, decides to come out of the closet as a gay man, could have been based on the life of Dahlia Stone. She was 67 when her husband died. She married her girlfriend, Sandra, five years later. Dahlia made a lot of money when she sold her family's consumer packaging company to a Fortune 500 company. She had taken over the family business when her father died 40 years earlier. Dahlia's three adult sons, Stephen, Jonathan, and Zachary, had some concerns that their mom's new spouse was after the family wealth. They urged her to sign a prenuptial agreement with Sandra, who was 15 years younger than Dahlia and had two adult daughters from her first marriage. Luckily, both Dahlia and Sandra saw the benefits of a prenuptial agreement. Dahlia wanted to protect her assets for her sons, while Sandra, who had a small but not very profitable invitation business, wanted some financial security as she aged.

A simple agreement was created. Sandra would receive $300,000 each year the couple remained married, as well as $2 million paid up front out of Dahlia's estate. Sandra could lay no claim to anything else in Dahlia's estate. That meant that Dahlia's home in Santa Fe and all its contents, as well as the remainder of her estate, could be left to her sons without conflict or question. It was a win-win for both sides of the family.

Prenuptial agreements are not the only asset-protection options available when blending families. Trusts, family limited liability companies (LLCs),[2] postnuptial agreements,[3] and disability and life insurance policies are other vehicles that can be used, depending on the financial situation of the soon-to-be-married partners.

In some jurisdictions, trusts that we create for our own benefit may provide protection against our creditors, including a divorcing spouse. The rules pertaining to these trusts are complex and vary from state to state (and country to country), and the advice of an expert attorney will be necessary.

Entities such as partnerships and LLCs may also provide some protection in the event of a divorce. It is generally possible to structure transfers to these entities so that they will be free of income tax or gift tax, but expert advice on these matters is essential. Although the LLC or partnership structure may provide enhanced protection in the event of a divorce, these methods are not fail-safe by any means. Among other things, it generally will be important to keep the ownership interests in the entities from being treated as marital property. But I cannot stress enough that the rules that apply in these areas are extremely complex and vary from state to state. At the end of the day, you will need expert advice.

Another asset-protection strategy to consider is a postnuptial agreement. Advisors often recommend this vehicle when a family member wants to transfer the ownership of a large asset, such as an interest in a family business. In my experience, when a spouse requests one, it is often a sign of a troubled marriage. But often a third party, such as another owner of the business, a trusted advisor, or even another family member, requests a postnuptial agreement as part of a larger family financial plan, independent of the marital relationship. These agreements can be delicate in nature, and, if not handled and constructed properly, can easily create irreparable conflict between the spouses. In order for the spouse to agree to relinquish interest in the large asset, she might have to be mollified by being given another asset to replace the one relinquished. And, in the event of divorce, these agreements can provide a road map for dissolution of the marital property and distribution of assets. Too often they turn into self-fulfilling prophecies.

Two planning vehicles that are commonly overlooked are disability and life insurance policies used in combination with pre- or postnuptial agreements. These policies provide financial protection in case a spouse becomes disabled or dies. Divorce decrees will often require life insurance to guarantee alimony or child support. Disability insurance should be considered as well, since the probability of disability is higher than that of death at almost every age. In any case, you need to evaluate all your insurance before and after a divorce, and before each marriage.

Asset protection is not the only financial and estate-planning strategy you will need to create when you blend families. Conflict lurks behind every corner in a blended family, and it is best to try to anticipate potholes before they appear. Family consolidations often come with some form of alimony and/or child support from previous marriages, as well as questions about where and with whom the children will live and where they will go to school. Will they attend public or private school? If there is a financial disparity in the family, who will pay for it? As the kids mature, there are ongoing expenses such as college and graduate school, along with living arrangements, to consider. Blended families with younger children will need to focus more on day-to-day decisions.

The Greenes, for example, needed to talk about who would be responsible for making the decisions regarding the children they brought to the new marriage. Would Julie and Barry make big decisions only for their own children or for each other's as well? When the ex-spouse is still in the picture, the scenario is much more complicated. Who will decide whether or not to let a child go on a school retreat? How and when will decisions be communicated to the parent who does not live with the child?

While child-rearing issues can be difficult to resolve, the most difficult conflicts in blended families arise over different values in families that have different histories, backgrounds, and cultures.

If you are combining two 56-year-olds, each with two adult kids, it is easy to imagine that each family brings longstanding values that may have been passed down from earlier generations of relatives who also had specific money values.

Consider a mother who has been financially capable of sending her children to a private school, taking them on expensive vacations, and giving them virtually everything they wanted and needed over many years. Then she marries her second husband. He is not nearly as wealthy as she is, and that is reflected in the way he has raised his kids. They worked for an allowance each week to pay for things they needed. They attended public school and did not travel very much as they were growing up. How can this couple handle the disparity in lifestyles and money values? It is almost as if two cultures are being merged. A clash in class and culture exists that needs to be addressed early and with frequent communication. It is a difficult task, often requiring advisors to help.

Stan Stringer was a very successful, athletic 58-year-old hedge fund manager in New York City. His father, who owned a retail chain in the Northeast, had passed away and left him a substantial sum of money. Stan's girlfriend of two years, Emily, a 56-year-old tall, blonde beauty with blue eyes, was ready for him to make a firmer commitment after they had been living together for a year. Emily was active in a start-up clothing design business to which she had committed some of her liquid resources. She was devoted to her two sons, Hank, who was a sophomore in college at Amherst, and Spencer, who was a junior in high school.

Stan also had been married before. He had an 18-year-old daughter, Elizabeth, who still lived with him, and a 23-year-old daughter, Sharon, who was in law school, and he wanted to protect them financially. He also had significant debt associated with his business and a second home in Aspen, Colorado. As a result, Stan was quite nervous about remarrying.

Both Stan and Emily shared their concerns with their financial advisor in separate meetings so that the advisor could get the full facts and stories from each. The advisor learned that Stan was more of a risk taker with investments than Emily, and that he was more comfortable with taking on debt. Emily was financially secure with a solid professional life. She would be able to take care of putting her kids through college and other expenses that might arise. However, when they started talking about a prenuptial agreement, there were some differences. No matter what Stan was prepared to carve out for Emily in the prenuptial agreement, she was not happy if it came with a large piece of his mounting debt. Through a number of meetings the advisor had with both of them, separately and together, they were able to help Stan understand Emily's concerns and the limitations of his assets.

Should Stan decide to retire early and maintain his healthy lifestyle, his objectives would need to be carefully reconsidered, particularly the risk of maintaining such a significant amount of debt associated with a business and a second home. Both Stan and Emily enjoyed international travel and wanted to continue traveling together often. A large part of the advisor's conversations with Stan centered on how to divide up his assets in a fair way that honored his commitment to Emily and her risk tolerance, while protecting his daughters. As part of those conversations, his investment mix was retooled in light of the new stage of life he was entering and the more conservative leaning of his new partner. He decided to significantly reduce his business debt and eliminate the debt on the Aspen home. He agreed to leave the second home in trust, along with the primary residence, to his new wife. He also established a life insurance trust[4] to use part of his current $5 million gift tax exclusion[5] to secure a chunk of assets for his daughters down the road.

In addition to negotiating handling the assets in a combined family scenario, cash flow and how to handle the kids' daily needs have to be agreed upon. Once again, the parties have to decide who is responsible for which expense, how much each child needs, what the family is willing to provide, and from which pot that money will be taken. Once the agreement is finalized, my recommendation has always been to put it in writing so that everyone is on the same page and there are no questions about responsibilities.

Financial circumstances can change with the wind. Just look back to the previous chapter if you need a reminder. A spouse may lose a job, experience a large failed investment, or see her business lose a major client. Regardless of the situation, it is essential to discuss the changing circumstances and, if necessary, amend any agreement.

That is what Jay McKay had to do when he recently remarried after leaving his first wife 16 years ago. His California-based construction company was hit hard by the real estate bust in his state, its struggling economy, and its higher than national average rate of unemployment. Jay was not able to continue the huge alimony and child support payments he was required to make as part of a divorce agreement drafted in very different economic times. He had recently gone back to court to request a reduction in the size of his payments. His ex-wife had been collecting rental income on new commercial properties that she had acquired with her new husband, a lawyer, who, independent of the circumstances of the divorced couple, was financially able to contribute to the family expenses. In addition, Jay spoke with his four children, three of whom were in college or graduate school, and explained that the cash flow was not going to be as robust. Although his kids were not destitute and could continue their college and graduate school educations without incurring debt, they were disappointed that their monthly allowances would be cut. Their mother also had to assume the cost of their medical and car expenses. Still, despite conflict and disappointment, the conversations were necessary, and the changes were warranted. With proper support and documentation, Jay was able to argue successfully for the alimony and child support reductions. Although his ex-wife was not happy with the judge's decision, she accepted the amendment to the divorce agreement because of the highly detailed substantiation that was presented.

Marital transitions, however beneficial they may be in the long run, are almost always emotionally anguishing in the short term. The distress and anxiety affect not just the two spouses, but their children and perhaps other members of the families. Understanding and disclosing information, conveyed in a caring Money Talk, can at least mitigate the short-term pain.

Things to Think About

- Blending families is difficult in the short and long term, not just logistically, but emotionally as well. What are the logistical issues you are facing? What are the emotional issues you are facing?
- Have a Money Talk as early as possible, and strive for full disclosure of not only your financial information but your attitudes and values about money. What does money mean to each of you? Power? Security? Something else?
- Are young children part of the blended family? If so, who will make decisions regarding them? Who will be responsible for their expenses? Are there differences in family cultures that could lead to conflict?
- Does one partner bring significantly more assets to the relationship than the other? If so, asset protection needs to be considered. This can be difficult and often requires the help of an unbiased advisor.
- Do not reflexively avoid prenuptial agreements. They can be structured so the fears and concerns of both parties are addressed, for example, through special distributions in the event of death or divorce.
- With professional guidance, consider alternative asset protection devices, such as trusts, family limited liability companies, postnuptial agreements, and disability and life insurance policies.

5

Retirement Planning

Having Money Talks About Saving and Investing for Life After Work

There is a kind of fear, approaching a panic, that's spreading through the Baby Boom Generation, which has suddenly discovered that it will have to provide for its own retirement.
—Ron Chernow

I watch the *Today Show* almost every morning and have been a fan of the show since the Hugh Downs days of my youth. I thoroughly enjoy the segments in which Willard Scott delivers his Smucker's-sponsored birthday tributes and wishes the smiling centenarians a happy birthday. I wonder if my name and picture will ever float across the *Today Show*, and what my lifestyle will be like if I reach the 100-year-old milestone. According to the Census Bureau, I have a pretty good chance. Centenarians are the fastest-growing segment of the population. And, many life insurance companies are extending their illustration systems to 120 years old to reflect the new reality of extended mortalities. According to the present mortality tables, those who were 75 in 2007 can expect to live to 86.7. While their health might be good, their finances are often in poor shape. Living beyond 100 years old is a very expensive proposition. For those of us who do not make it to triple digits, just reaching the average life expectancy may put a strain on our personal finances.

In addition to the uncertainty associated with your life expectancy, or the longevity risk, the other element that can derail your retirement is inflation. One of the most important questions to ask when you become dependent for income on your investment assets, your retirement plans, and social security is, what is your particular inflation rate? Individual inflation rates are often much higher than what the government reports as "core" inflation, since that excludes energy, food, and other essential expenses. The costs of energy and healthcare, for example, have been rising at rates far above the core inflation rate, which is about 2 percent as of the writing of this book. Then there is the cost of food, which is rising at 4 percent.

There is an interesting trend in attitudes toward retirement. It is well documented that the largest demographic, the 77 million baby boomers who represent 26 percent of the nation's population, is marching in large numbers toward the magic age of 65. Between January 1 and December 31, 2011, 7,000 people turned 65 each day, according to the American Association of Retired Persons (AARP) Turning 65 Survey. But many boomers, particularly those who love what they do, intend to work well beyond the retirement age of their parents' generation. According to a January 2011 Merrill Lynch Affluent Insights Survey, an estimated 70 percent of boomers plan to keep working at least part time during their "retirement" years. Perhaps this is because boomers cannot envision themselves as not having an active life for the next 30 years. Or maybe it is because the past decade plus of difficult economic and market periods has convinced them that they will have to continue to work beyond the normal retirement age to support their lifestyles.

This means that this generational cohort, which has redefined so many parts of life and significantly affected the economy in the process, will be doing the same thing with aging and retirement. Many boomers in their fifties and older are choosing new professions, or encore careers. Bestselling author Gail Sheehy calls the period between 45 and 65 a second adulthood rather than middle or old age. The Merrill Lynch survey reports that 26 percent of aging baby boomers plan to continue their education, 24 percent are looking to learn a new trade, and 20 percent plan to start a new business. According to psychologist Ken Dychtwald, chief executive officer of Age Wave, Inc., a California-based consulting firm, because boomers are living longer, healthier lives, they are able to rethink retirement and turn it into mini-retirements that are dotted with career shifts, part-time or flextime work, entrepreneurial endeavors, and continued education.

Technology is also making it easier for people to combine work or running their own business with other activities, such as traveling or having more free time. People can have web-based virtual meetings, use the Internet to communicate around the world, and access information and work online.

As it turns out, learning something new, such as the ever-changing technology options, and remaining engaged in life causes your brain to create new pathways. While neuroplasticity, as it is known, is a crucial part of recovery for anyone who loses a sense or a cognitive or motor ability, it can also be a vital part of everyone's daily life. Dr. Oliver Sacks, a neurologist and author of *The Mind's Eye*, among other books, noted in a January 1, 2011, *New York Times* Op-Ed piece that our brain never stops growing. "Every time we practice an old skill or learn a new one, existing neural connections are strengthened and, over time, neurons create more connections to other neurons. Even new nerve cells can be generated." So whether you learn a new language, travel to a new place, or learn a new skill, each of these activities will stimulate your brain to grow. You might call it cognitive fitness.

There are plenty of emotional and mental reasons to remain engaged in the workplace—maintaining your mental acuity, reducing loneliness, and retaining a sense of purpose and accomplishment. But for many, the underlying reason to continue working longer is financial. With yields on short-term money at historical lows, the S&P 500 flat for the decade between 2000 and 2010, uncertainty about future market returns, unprecedented volatility in the markets, and life expectancies extending way beyond what had been anticipated by our parents' generation, the baby boomers have reason to worry. Their very real fear is that they are not going to have enough money to live out their lives and that there will be nothing left for their children. I think Johann Wolfgang von Goethe, the brilliant nineteenth-century German polymath, best summed up the prevailing investor psychology with his phrase "heavenly joy, deadly sorrow."

Stories abound of already retired individuals who are rightfully nervous. Many have had to trim their lifestyles because of loss of principal[1] during the severe economic and market downturn of 2008–2009. As a result, their investment income and earnings are significantly lower than they expected. Many parents have undergone a reversal of fortunes, but have hidden the downfall rather than share it with their children. They may be embarrassed or fear that if their children know of their financial change, they will feel that they need to support their parents, which will create more anxiety for the family. Because of some families' lack of disclosure, adult children have unrealistic expectations of what they will receive as an inheritance. Others may be worried about the decimation of their expected inheritance because of the risky economy and world markets. These worries are more prevalent among children in families with less than $10 million than in families with more significant wealth.

As a result, clients are revisiting their financial plans with their advisors. I have noticed an increase in requests from clients to meet more frequently and to address issues involving retirement. In these meetings with individual clients, we have been consolidating retirement assets and reviewing estate planning for possible simplification, such as terminating trusts or changing gifting policies. We have also been taking a closer look at possible changes in their investment strategy, such as seeking investments that create more income and have a more conservative risk profile. I have used one particular strategy with families that are worried that their spending habits will lead them to consuming their assets and leaving their heirs with less than they planned. We create an insurance trust and typically fund it with a guaranteed universal life insurance policy.[2] By doing this, monies are set aside for the children, and the parents can worry less about the money they are spending during their life-time. In fact, a popular planning vehicle among the ultra-wealthy is to use the maximum existing federal gift tax exclusion to fund large insurance policies for the children's benefit.[3]

In the context of the "new normal" financial environment, every family member needs to rethink and revisit financial expectations tied to her plans for the future. That means that the big, looming elephant in the room, the M Word conversation, has to be tackled. Family members need to talk about the assets they own, where those assets are located, whether they are protected in the event of the owner's death and disability, where the legal documents are, how much they are spending, and how, in the context of retirement planning, they can better manage their money to reach their goals. Outliving retirement savings is not just about you—it is about the entire family.

That is how the Stoddards approached their situation. In contrast to the steep divorce rates I noted earlier, Mona and James Stoddard are happily married after 40 years together in a New Jersey suburb, raising three kids. James, a portly 66-year-old with wire-rim glasses who was a successful corporate attorney with a major law firm, had retired from his practice in April 2007, just before the market tanked. Mona, a heavyset 64-year-old woman with jade green eyes, decided to retire at the same time after spending 30 years teaching music theory at a local university.

Upon her retirement, Mona decided to take two monthly retirement distributions: one from her 403(b) plan and another from her university pension, which was annually restated and adjusted based on a market performance formula. James had a 401(k)[4] and a profit-sharing plan[5] that he rolled into an IRA. Like many male investors, when he left his firm, he was heavily invested in risky assets, such as equities and hedge funds, and was not adequately diversified. When the market took a deep downturn, James lost a significant portion of his portfolio while simultaneously taking large IRA withdrawals.

Like millions of other stock market investors, Mona found that the restated value of her retirement account as of 12/31/2008 was significantly lower than it had been the previous year. This resulted in a lower-than-expected annual pension amount paid out to her and her husband. While they had suspected that the market meltdown would lower their retirement income, neither Mona nor James was prepared for the huge hit they suddenly took. And, their projected income needs that were at risk extended to their responsibility for caring for Mona's mother. Almost 90, she currently lives a relatively healthy life in a local assisted-living facility, which is quite expensive. The couple knew that at some point, if she ran through her funds, they might need to supplement the monthly expense of her care or even meet it in its entirety. Longevity runs in the family. Mona and James both realized that, given the current market environment, they were not going to be able to keep up the currently scheduled amount of retirement and other income distributions from their assets, including some inherited monies, for the long term. Suddenly they felt the very real fear of outliving their money.

For the first time, Mona and James were nervous about being able to maintain their longstanding lifestyle and also continue to care for their children and grandchildren and their community. They had always believed in helping their adult children financially whenever they could. Each year they had made a tax-free gift to each child and grandchild. Although it was not the maximum allowed under the law, it was quite helpful and paid for some of the children's household and education expenses. When their adult children needed extra money for down payments on their homes or other family-related expenses, Mona and James took pride in being able to provide cash loans at low interest rates. They did not just enjoy giving to their children and grandchildren. The couple had always been charitably minded. They were increasingly concerned that they would have to scale back the financial support they had given to their community over the years.

Unfortunately, the couple did not have anyone with whom to discuss these new financial developments. Rather than working with an advisor, they had always done their own investing. For many years, it had worked. Now, with the uncertainty of the markets and their increasing fears about whether or not they would have enough money to manage their personal expenses and continue their family and charitable commitments, they agreed that it was time to talk to a financial counselor. Once they made the decision, they began the intensive process of interviewing different advisors to help them sort it out. They entered my office with their hands full of statements and documents and a long list of concerns.

After I reviewed all their liquid and nonliquid assets,[6] I reconstructed the Stoddards's portfolio. Luckily, they had purchased permanent insurance in life insurance trusts that were fully funded. At least they knew that their children would have a decent lump sum to pay their estate taxes and be distributed to their heirs. I took into account their combined growth and income objectives, risk tolerances, and time horizons, while considering what they said they needed each year in order to live. With that amount in mind, we determined a reasonable monthly withdrawal amount that I thought could be sustained over the next 30 years, adjusted for inflation. As you might guess, it was not the monthly amount they had hoped for, or the amount they were used to. But it gave them a set of guidelines. With this road map in hand, their financial paralysis ebbed, and the Stoddards began to make other decisions about employment, gifting, and charitable donations.

One decision was whether or not James would return to work. He was a very talented attorney who had worked closely with some important clients, and his firm had not wanted him to retire. The managing partner was looking to pass the baton, and James had significant managerial skills. Like many retirees who had experienced financial setbacks, it occurred to James that he might want to go back to work until he and his wife had a better handle on their finances and could manage their financial commitments more easily. Taking all of these considerations into account, James decided to return to work part time for the next five years as the firm's new managing director at a healthy, but reduced, salary. This would give the couple's portfolio time to recover and potentially grow. It also meant that they would not have to use the maximum amount from their retirement plans and could build up the balance through new contributions and potential growth.

Perhaps the most challenging aspect of this financial reset was speaking to their children. They needed their children to take a more active role in financing their own children's needs and paying for their current education. As you might imagine, that was not an easy conversation for anyone. First they discussed the change in their financial affairs with each child individually, and then as a family.

There is more to planning for retirement than numbers. Most people overlook the psychological impact of this transition. We are all so engaged in our work lives that we do not have the emotional energy or the time to think about what we will do if and when we choose to stop working. Even those of us who swear that we will leave our offices only on a stretcher need to do some psychological preparation for slowing down or shifting gears.

Just as there are specific guidelines for preparing your financial portfolio, there are ways to prepare your psychological portfolio, says Nancy K. Schlossberg, an expert in the area of adult transitions and a professor emerita, Department of Counseling and Personnel Services, College of Education at the University of Maryland. She identifies three legs to your psychological portfolio. First, you will need to think about your identity. How will you identify yourself once you are retired? What will be your personal elevator speech— your 30-second introduction about yourself—once you move out of the workforce? Second, you will need to prepare for the change in your professional relationships. Many of them will change dramatically and will erode over time, says Schlossberg. And third, there must be a passion piece for your twilight years. What will get you up in the morning each day and give meaning and purpose to your life?

If you plan for both the psychological and the financial aspects of retirement, you will be better equipped and able to create and enjoy a phase of life that is as enriching and as memorable as the earlier growth phases.

Things to Think About

- Have you considered the impact inflation and potentially longer life spans will have on your retirement investments and plan?
- There are emotional and mental as well as financial reasons to consider alternatives to the traditional full retirement, such as career shifts, part-time work, flex-time work, entrepreneurial ventures, and further education.
- Has the recent economic downturn seriously impacted your retirement investments and plans? If so, have you discussed the impact with family members who may be making their own plans based on a mistaken assumption of likely inheritances?
- Think about nonfinancial issues as well. What will be your identity if you stop working at your current job? How will your work-centered relationships change? What will give purpose to your life when you are retired?

6

Caring for an Elderly Parent

Having Money Talks About Parents' Long-Term Care

A test of a people is how it behaves toward the old. It is easy to love children. Even tyrants and dictators make a point of being fond of children. But the affection and care for the old, the incurable, the helpless are the true gold mines of a culture.
—Abraham J. Heschel

Take good notes and do a caring, thoughtful job if you are parenting your parents. You will want your kids to have a good road map for taking care of you if and when that time comes.

As the elderly population continues to increase, so do people's concerns about caring for those they love who are elderly. Today approximately 10 million Americans need long-term-care services, ranging from weekly visits by a home health aide to permanent round-the-clock care in a nursing home. As the baby boomers age, it is expected that 15 million older Americans will need long-term care by 2020, reported Kathy Greenlee, assistant secretary for aging, U.S. Department of Health and Human Services, in a March 2011 statement before a congressional subcommittee.

Most aging Americans are cared for in the comfort of their own homes. Family and friends are the sole caregivers for 70 percent of the elderly. However, anyone who reaches 65 years old has a

40 percent chance of entering a nursing home and a 20 percent chance of staying there for five years or more, according to Greenlee. And the prospect of paying for it can be daunting. The average annual cost for a room in a nursing home is about $75,000, and it can exceed $100,000 in some parts of the country. In fact, one out of six people who reach the age of 65 will spend more than $100,000 annually on long-term care, according to Greenlee. She added that 22 percent of those who enter a nursing home exhaust their own resources and eventually qualify for Medicaid. She noted that only about 8 to 10 percent of Americans have private long-term-care insurance[1] coverage.

Many of us, even if there are sufficient family financial resources or long-term-care insurance is in place, find that it is incredibly challenging and sometimes overwhelming to manage the emotional issues that come with the long-term care of a friend, family member, or partner. Many of the 44 million American families and friends who provide unpaid care to another adult are at risk of mental, emotional, and physical health problems resulting from the strain, according to the Family Caregiver Alliance. In one of its surveys, 17 percent of caregivers thought their own health had gotten worse as a result of their caregiving responsibilities. That percentage jumped to 23 percent for those who had been providing care for five years or longer. And it is not just physical problems that plague caregivers. According to the Family Caregiver Alliance, about 60 percent have clinically significant symptoms of depression.

What is the best way to minimize the physical, emotional, and mental strain? Accepting that supporting an aging parent is not a one-person job. In my experience, one adult child steps forward and takes on the major responsibility of parenting the elderly parent, from making sure that the day-to-day physical care is sufficient to overseeing financial affairs. In some families, there is a well-thought-out division of duties between family members based on who has the skills to deal with the issues and who is willing and able to make the commitment. In other situations, the care just falls to the adult child who is geographically closest to the parent. If there is no one nearby to care for the aging parent, if there is no family member with the necessary skills, or if there is no one who is acceptable to all the family members, the family must consider a third party for the leadership position.

Even if there is a family member who is ready, willing, and able to provide care, having a third party available can be a great help. David Darst, managing director and chief investment strategist for Morgan Stanley, calls this person an "Uncle Frank." In his book *The Little Book That Saves Your Assets*, he writes that an Uncle Frank (or an Aunt Sally) is someone that everyone in the family trusts implicitly who is prepared to help with big decisions. He may have helped family members make important decisions in the past, is not envious, has no sibling rivalry, is comfortable with himself, and can provide mental and emotional support to the family. This person could be a cousin, a niece, a close family friend, or a coworker. It is usually not a spouse. Sometimes it is a trustee of a family trust or a professional advisor to the family, such as an attorney or accountant. The family can select an Uncle Frank informally, or that person can be identified in legal documents that have been carefully crafted and executed for such situations.

It is important to understand, however, that even if you are the family point person, and even if you have an Uncle Frank, you can ask for help from other family members. The bottom line is that everyone needs to work together as a team. When your family team adds the right advisors, from physical and emotional healthcare practitioners—such as a primary-care physician, a geriatrician, medical specialists, a nutritionist, mental health professionals, and a geriatric-care manager—to a trusted cadre of financial and legal experts, you will be well supported and more likely be able to safeguard yourself against caregiver burnout.

With a trusted team in place, you will be better prepared to handle the increasingly stressful steps that come fast and furiously as a person ages. The time may come when the team or a chosen or self-selected member of the family needs to choose the right facility for your loved one. This could be a long process that includes drawing up a list of various options, visiting them all, and ensuring their availability at the necessary time. A wide range of options exist when it comes to settling on a place where your aging relative can live out her last days. However, most elderly people want to stay in their homes. Choosing among assisted-living facilities and nursing homes is not only about finding the right physical place, but also about selecting the right professionals who can care for your elderly relative and her specific issues. You will want to ask friends and acquaintances who have successfully dealt with these elder-care issues for referrals of well-respected places and professionals. This can be a long and arduous process, but it is important that you get it right. Again, enlist siblings or friends to make the rounds with you to help you evaluate the various facilities.

Richard Reed, 76, a writer living in Washington, DC, has tried twice to move his father, Earl, into an assisted-living facility. Earl, a feisty 98-year-old with a mane of white hair, still lives in the house in Kenosha, Wisconsin, where Richard grew up. Both times, Earl moved into a facility and then moved back home a week later. Richard was looking for an easier alternative. Even though Richard's cousin, a nurse who lives in Kenosha, stopped by every week to check on Earl, it was getting increasingly difficult for Richard to manage the 24-hour care of his father and his around-the-clock home health aides. Richard accepted the fact that Earl was never going to leave his own home. Although his cousin was available and he traveled frequently to Kenosha to check on his dad, Richard decided to hire a local geriatric-care manager to oversee Earl's day-to-day care.

Geriatric-care managers are licensed social workers, counselors, nurses, gerontologists, or psychologists with expertise in elder-care issues. Not only are they able to help with medical and emotional challenges, but they are also able to deal with the logistical and interpersonal issues that arise. Their services range from helping families navigate insurance policies, acting as advocates at hospitals and nursing homes, arranging for in-home care and home modifications, monitoring medications, and finding lawyers for legal problems to taking people to medical appointments and traveling with them. Additionally, geriatric-care managers have access to inside knowledge on everything from the quality of local facilities and in-home services and where to find medical equipment and supplies to unadvertised benefits offered by various local and national associations and organizations, such as the Veterans Administration.

While they are often appointed when families are geographically distant from an aging relative, geriatric-care managers can also be tremendous assets for local family caregivers. An estimated 50 percent of those 85 and older suffer from cognitive impairment. Geriatric-care managers can objectively identify cognitive problems. When a family member is having difficulty understanding what the doctor is saying, a geriatric-care manager can serve as an interpreter. These professionals can stay above the emotional turmoil. They can also provide assistance in determining an annual budget to care for the elderly parent and project the cost of making home improvements so that the aging relative can stay at home. It is often more affordable and practical for families to hire geriatric-care managers than to travel frequently to deal with the issues surrounding elderly loved ones.

Most important, the support of a geriatric-care manager allows adult children to continue the routines of their personal lives, while still staying involved with their parents. Time with mom or dad becomes bonding time, rather than a visit that leaves everyone stressed and feeling helpless when facing the aging experience. Most long-term-care insurance providers will hire a care-management company to oversee the care a person is receiving through a long-term-care policy. It is a way of making sure that the relationship is free of abuse, both physically and financially, and can provide a level of comfort to families that any issues that arise are being identified and reported.

If your relative is a feisty elderly individual like Earl, it is important that you explore the stay-home option fully. It is not necessarily difficult or expensive to adapt homes to the special needs of aging individuals. Just as caretakers can be hired to help new parents make sure their adorable infant is safe and is not going to knock over bookshelves or fall down the stairs, professionals can be hired to add a chair lift on the stairs or special bars and handles in the bathroom so that a home is safer for an elderly person. Some long-term-care insurance policies cover home modifications. If you make improvements that do not increase the value of the home, you may be able to deduct those modifications as medical expenses. You can hire a geriatric consultant or a social worker to file a report that can be attached to your tax return.

For companionship, there are community-based senior centers with activity-filled daycare programs. Transportation to and from the center is often available. If 24-hour care is not necessary, families can contract for a visiting nurse service or a doctor who makes house calls to make regular visits.

A friend of mine, Gail Rafferty, recently built a fully functional downstairs living space for her 87-year-old mother, Ida. Gail, an affable and optimistic 44-year-old schoolteacher, lives in part of the downstairs and all of the second floor of her suburban New York City home with her two middle-school-aged children, Sam and Gillian, and her husband, Todd, an ex-professional baseball player turned mortgage broker. A year ago, Ida fell and broke her hip. It was assumed that Gail, the only daughter of four adult children and the one who lived closest to Ida, would care for her. Gail decided that the best option for her aging mother was to have her live with Gail's family—separately but together. By the time Ida's hip healed, she needed 24-hour home healthcare. Her living downstairs made it easier for Gail, Todd, or one of the kids to drop in throughout the day to make sure that all her needs were being met. Gail contracted for a daily meal service so that she would not be responsible for her mother's meals.

Finding the right living situation for an elderly relative only ensures that his physical needs are met. Once those decisions have been made, you next need to manage the legal and financial issues and make sure the necessary documents are executed and accessible to everyone who needs to see them. For this, you will need to tap a trusted financial advisor, accountant, attorney, or all three. There is a lot of paperwork involved, and everything has to be done properly, or else it can potentially result in disaster for the elderly relative. Stories abound of elder-care fraud, either as a result of untrustworthy individuals being appointed to financial decision-making positions, incompetent individuals being left to care for the ailing family member with no supervision, or the aging individual making poor decisions as a result of cognitive impairment.

One of my clients had to take over the financial affairs of his 80-year-old mother quickly when he discovered that she had lent money to a distant relative for a real estate investment without any documentation and without understanding the risks. She was in charge of her own financial affairs at the time, and there was no one to provide checks and balances for her increasingly erratic financial behavior. She was subsequently diagnosed with Alzheimer's disease. My client had no recourse on the real estate investment, which had gone bad, and was unable to recover the lost funds. While there are documents that can help protect your elderly relative from such situations, it is ultimately up to you and your family members to be on the lookout for cognitive decline and make sure that documents are created in time to take any necessary legal actions. My client had not preemptively created the documents that would have allowed him to step in and protect his mother's finances.

A power of attorney[2] with a durable power of attorney[3] clause included is the most essential of these documents. It appoints someone to handle the legal, tax, and financial affairs of an individual who cannot perform those duties. It could be that the person is not able to be physically present, that she is in some way unable to represent herself as a result of physical or mental incapacity, or both. If your relative already has a health issue, you might want to have a tailored power of attorney crafted that covers specific health needs. When there is no power of attorney in place, the court will appoint a stranger who may not have your relative's best interest at heart.

Be aware, however, that if the power of attorney is not durable, it will be valid only under certain circumstances. If your relative becomes incapacitated, you may suddenly find yourself without the necessary legal rights to care for him. All that is required to make the power of attorney durable is the following language: "This power of attorney shall not terminate in the event of my disability." A durable power of attorney is a permanent, all-encompassing legal vehicle that gives broad-reaching power. You could also draft a temporary limited power of attorney[4] for instances when a relative is traveling outside the country and needs someone to pay his bills for a period of time.

A durable power of attorney has to be executed in a thoughtful way, with a trustworthy person in charge, so that the document does what it is supposed to do. A niece who is up against a foreclosure on her home would clearly not be the best person to be given a durable power of attorney. Pick a responsible person who can keep the lines of communication among the family members open. You might want to appoint a trusted attorney or accountant as a coagent in situations where you anticipate abuse or in which family relations are strained. However, if you take this avenue, then both coagents will have to sign off on any requests or changes. That may seem like a good idea initially, but if one of the coagents is skiing in Utah, it might be difficult to track her down and get a required signature.

Draft your own power of attorney for your later years while you are still healthy and still have your full faculties, and encourage your aging relative to do the same thing. It is important to have the opportunity to review your loved one's documents while he is healthy. When drawing up the power of attorney, you might think about including an amendment that includes the ability to hire and use a geriatric-care manager.

You will also want to have a healthcare proxy[5] that allows an individual or individuals to make healthcare decisions for a person who is incapacitated. Attorneys often mix up the healthcare proxy and the power of attorney and call it a healthcare power of attorney. But make no mistake; there are no financial powers included in a healthcare proxy. Most hospitals and healthcare facilities, including those that provide long-term care, require these documents to be on file with them.

You will also want to ensure that your elderly relative has a living will.[6] This is an expression of the kinds of care and treatment your relative wishes at the end of life and reflects, for the family, what is important to the individual who is incapacitated and is facing end-of-life issues.

Finally, you will also need a Health Insurance Portability and Accountability Act (HIPPA)[7] release. Say your mom is going in for surgery. You may need to tap into your mother's health records. You will not be able to do this unless you have had her sign a HIPPA release.

Trusts are a versatile vehicle that can help prevent elder-care abuse and protect your aging relative's assets if there is a real or perceived threat to the family's financial security. In certain circumstances, a trust can reduce the need for a power of attorney. I wrote about the use of trusts in the discussion of blending families in Chapter 4, and I will revisit them in the next chapter when I discuss transferring assets across generations and preparing heirs. If a spouse is still healthy—both physically and mentally—then she can serve as trustee. What often happens, however, is that a surviving spouse is not able to handle the day-to-day decisions or act as trustee. In that case, advisors often recommend that the spouse resign and appoint a successor trustee.[8] It is helpful to include a cotrustee arrangement so that you are prepared if the surviving spouse is unwilling to give up control. This can help to protect the family assets and give everyone a certain peace of mind.

Mary Nelson, an 85-year-old widow, was a vital and spunky woman for most of her life. She raised two wonderful children, or so she thought until she started to have some physical and mental issues. Her husband, a very successful workaholic entrepreneur, had died of heart disease five years earlier after multiple bypass surgeries. He left Mary quite comfortable financially. She lived independently in an upscale two-bedroom condo on a golf course in Palm Beach, Florida. Her oldest child, Jenna, lived nearby with her family. Her son, Connor, still single, visited often from his home in Boston.

Mary's attorney and her kids started to see changes in Mary's behavior and her mental acuity. She could not remember meeting the attorney, even though they had met several times before, and she had forgotten to attend a confirmed meeting that had been scheduled weeks earlier. Mary was starting to realize that her memory was not what it used to be, but she still had good analytic capability, and she refused to acknowledge any decrease in her mental capacity. She would often get worried, almost panicked, about her finances, fearing that the monies were not there. Her husband had tried to get Mary to take on financial responsibility when he was beginning to fail, but she was not interested. It was not surprising that in meetings with her advisors and her children, Mary demonstrated terrible insecurity. She refused to allow planning that would have put her financial fears at ease. She did not want to give up financial control, and because of her lack of knowledge, increasing insecurity, and decreasing mental acuity, she began to trust the wrong people. She refused to work with the investment advisors her attorney and accountant had selected. She found it easier to defer to family members who were not qualified or to let a friend who did not have the necessary skills educate her.

If Mary had listened to her husband and his advisors while she was in her sixties and still mentally and physically healthy, then she would have been able to learn about financial matters from competent teachers. Unfortunately, as happens all too often with women who have deferred to spouses or others on financial matters, she took control of her finances only when she was forced to by her husband's death. Had Mary lost her husband sooner, she might have learned what she needed to before she did some foolish things with her money. She purchased a piece of property in Florida from a company that went bankrupt and was unable to make good on its promises. She handed a large chunk of money to a very aggressive money manager who subsequently lost most of it with aggressive derivative vehicles and fraudulent reporting. She was forgetting to pay bills. When her daughter, Jenna, was visiting one weekend, she went through the bills and found multiple overdue notices and credit agency letters. Jenna realized that it was time to have a conversation with her brother, Connor, and the family attorney.

Unfortunately, Jenna and Connor were not on the same page when it came to the physical or financial care of their mother. Jenna was the primary caregiver and had her mom's interest at heart. Connor, who was a spendthrift and had little patience with his mom's care, had a bad habit of making poor business investments. He relied on his mother's largesse to support his over-the-top lifestyle and poor investments. Connor wanted his mom to continue her generous handouts, and, unfortunately, Mary had a blind spot for her younger child.

Given Mary's rapidly declining health, Jenna and Connor scheduled a meeting with the financial advisor to discuss what steps they should take. Should they let Mary have a checking account to give her some control, and if so, how much should be in it? But there were bigger issues at stake. How should they plan for Mary's continued decline in health, where should she live, and how should they manage the assets that Mary was incapable of handling on her own?

Before his death, Mary and her husband had created a revocable trust in her name and for her benefit. It needed to be funded, but unfortunately, Connor was designated as the successor trustee. At Jenna's request, the attorney and the accountant began to have in-depth conversations with Mary. She was currently designated as the trustee, and they encouraged her to step down and either name a new trustee or have Connor serve as cotrustee along with someone else. Mary did not want to give up control. However, after careful, repeated conversations with Jenna and the attorney, Mary understood that she needed to step down, given her declining capacity. The attorney, whom Mary began to trust and who was able to help her see her son's limitations as well as her own, would serve as a cotrustee with Connor. The attorney had also cleverly drafted a separate agreement that allowed for a makeup provision[9] at Mary's death for all the extra gifting that had been made to Connor over the course of his life.

Mary wanted to continue to live at home in her condo, although it was clear that she needed assistance with the activities of daily living. With the help of a geriatric-care manager, Jenna began to make inquiries about home healthcare aides who could help her mom and make her condo more senior-friendly. Fortunately, her father had purchased a long-term-care insurance policy, so 80 percent of the cost of aides—up to a maximum dollar amount over the next five years—was covered. Even some of the home improvements would be covered. The story had a relatively happy ending thanks to advisors who played the critical role of sorting out issues for the family.

Of course, you cannot just go marching off and make decisions for your elderly relative without his agreement or knowledge. There is a logistical side to managing these transitions, which we have just covered, and then there are the conversations that must take place to ensure that the changes take place smoothly, which we will soon cover. A quick point: one way to facilitate these conversations is to focus on the need to update legal documents once a year. Estate-planning experts stress the importance of reviewing plans annually and discussing who has the copies and where they are located. These annual meetings provide a great opportunity to either begin or follow up on discussions with your parents across a whole range of topics, including their health.

Things to Think About

- Caring for an aging relative is a daunting task, both emotionally and financially. This is not something you have to, or should, do on your own. Are there other family members who can help? If not, there are professionals to whom you can turn.
- Is there a member of the extended family, or a trusted advisor, who can serve as a sounding board and consultant when making major decisions?
- What are the various tasks that need to be done, and are there family members who are uniquely or specially qualified to take on any of these tasks? Or do you need to turn to an advisor for help?
- What are the members you will need on your caregiving team? Will you need physical and emotional healthcare practitioners, such as a primary-care physician, a geriatrician, medical specialists, a nutritionist, a mental health professional, and/or a geriatric-care manager? Do you have a trusted cadre of financial and legal experts?

(continued)

- Reach out for advice and guidance on all the options when considering the best housing options for an aging relative. Make sure that everyone has a chance to evaluate any facilities considered.
- Is distance an obstacle? If so, a geriatric-care manager can deal with logistic and interpersonal issues in your stead.
- Even if distance is not a problem, consider engaging a geriatric-care manager to help review the options and navigate the system.
- Is there a family member or a trusted professional in a position of oversight to ensure that cognitive issues and resulting problems, both physical and financial, are addressed quickly so there is no lasting damage?
- Are all the financial and legal documents in place so that the aging relative can maintain independence as long as possible, yet be protected if cognitive issues develop? These include a power of attorney with a durable power of attorney clause included, a healthcare proxy, a living will, and a HIPPA release.
- If there is sufficient time, trusts can be created to provide financial protection for the aging relative and the rest of the family.

Preparing Heirs, Estate Transfers, and Business Successions

Having Money Talks About Intergenerational Family Wealth

Another good thing about being poor is that when you are seventy your children will not have declared you legally insane in order to gain control of your estate.
—Woody Allen

Whenever I told people I was writing a book about money, family, and communication, the topic of wealth transfer and preparing heirs garnered the most interest. Whether I was speaking with acquaintances, friends, family, or professionals, the conversation typically morphed into a discussion of how to let kids know that the family has wealth and how to raise financially responsible children. It is something that everyone thinks about. I recall seeing the actor Hugh Grant being interviewed on the *Today Show* about his becoming a father for the first time. He talked about how one of the things he was most concerned about was how to ensure that his daughter was comfortable and had everything she needed, but that she did not have so much and expect so much that she would be demotivated in life.

These have always been important questions, but the need to address them, to educate family members and have in-depth conversations about the family money, has never been more compelling and necessary. It is estimated that more than $15 trillion will be transferred to the next generation between 2007 and 2026 and more than $59 trillion between 2007 and 2061, according to the wealth growth and transfer model constructed by John Havens and Paul Schervish of the Center on Wealth and Philanthropy at Boston College. Unfortunately, not all of it will successfully make it from the hands of one generation to the hands of the next. There is a 70 percent failure rate worldwide when transferring family wealth from one generation to another, according to studies by MIT, *The Economist,* and most recently a study by Roy Williams and Vic Preisser, authors of *Preparing Heirs: Five Steps to a Successful Transition of Family Wealth and Values.* Williams and Preisser examined the long-term effects of the wealth transfers of 3,250 families. Failure was defined as loss of control of assets through mismanagement, poor investments, or the like. As we mentioned in Chapter 1, the most common factor in these failures, cited as the primary cause of 60 percent of them, is a breakdown in communication and trust within the family unit.

One of my goals in this book is to facilitate conversations about money, particularly in the context of transferring assets across generations. I want families to have the skills to begin and continue to have healthy and productive conversations concerning money; conversations that nurture trust and positive family values, and that help prepare heirs. I want my readers to be in the 30 percent of families who are successful in transferring their assets. My hope is to give families a robust framework for discussion and dialogue. Once families start to have successful communications, I believe the pattern can become part of the family culture. And once it is part of a family's culture, that pattern can be passed on to future generations as well.

There is a good reason that sports analogies are so common: they tend to work. So forgive me in advance for using one here. Transferring wealth from one generation to another can be viewed as a team sport. The family is the team management: the owner, the general manager, and the head coach. The team's players are the accountant, the attorney, the financial/investment advisor, and the trustees or other fiduciaries. Just as the team management needs to make draft picks, trades, and free agent signings carefully, families need to assess and pick the right professionals, not only for their individual talents, but for how they will work together. Once the players are out on the field, the only way the team can succeed is through constant communication back and forth between the team management and the players. The family must be able to communicate well and direct the professionals. And someone in the family needs to take a leadership role in orchestrating the process.

Martin Shenkman, a prominent trust and estate attorney and prolific author with whom I often work, says that estate planning is not about transferring wealth but about transferring values. I could not agree more. There are family values questions that wealthy families need to ask when they are planning on transferring assets. How will money affect the professional drive of the next generation? What will be the impact of wealth on their communities and lifestyles?

I know of a Manhattan-based group named Tiger 21, made up of wealthy individuals with investable assets north of $10 million, that meets monthly. Many of the group's daylong meetings focus on how to manage the impact of wealth on their families: how to raise ambitious and charitable kids, and how much money to pass on versus how much to donate to organizations. While these individuals have frequent peer-to-peer meetings, I believe these kinds of conversations eventually need to include the kids. If you talk to your kids and prepare them, as I am trying to help you do in this book, you will have a much better chance to transfer monies successfully without significant financial loss.

While it may be hard to believe, many of these failures occur because families do not do enough to prepare their heirs. It is as if they are giving a 16-year-old the keys to a car without ever giving him a driving lesson. Imagine that teenager on the road, behind the wheel of an incredibly powerful machine. Being unprepared to inherit money will not kill someone directly. But in the absence of adequate learning and experience, it can certainly wreak immense emotional, mental, and financial destruction.

In part, families avoid preparing heirs because they believe that when they start to talk about money, they are really talking about death. Nobody wants to go there. The kids see their wealthy parents as a financial safety net that will always be there, which may not be the case. The parents are equally uncomfortable with the topic of death and don't want to confront their own mortality. They also may not want their kids to know about the money, fearing that if they do, they will lose their motivation and drive. Parents may also be conflicted about how to deal with the taboo subject matter with their family. Because of the inevitable lack of communication that results, parents worry that their children will be irresponsible, that they are naïve about the value of the money, and that they will not be prepared to inherit it and, as a result, will make some messy mistakes. These are some of the reasons why, when Williams and Preisser, the authors of *Preparing Heirs*, consult with wealthy families, they bring the entire family into the discussion. To that end, Williams and Preisser have developed a robust process that allows them to answer the question: "Are the members of your family prepared to make the transition?" They give every family member a 50-question family readiness survey. Each family member is asked to rate how much she agrees with statements such as: "Our family has well-understood rules with respect to family ownership of assets versus spousal ownership of assets"; "Heirs actively participate, and are heard, as our family evaluates its mission, our estate plan, and their future roles"; and "Our family members trust one another." The report that results from the survey is a comparison of a family's responses to the responses they have gleaned from affluent families who have successfully transferred their estates. A financial advisor, like myself, typically administers the survey and reviews the results with the family.

At the very least, this exercise helps the family understand the work that needs be done and helps to avoid some common disputes. One of the most common conflicts I see among family members arises when they are probating an estate. Before the details of the will are disclosed, I often witness the adult children imagining something far worse or far better than what is actually in the will. Why? Because their parents never discussed the contents of the will with them before they died. That is a big mistake. Whether or not the children all get exactly the same inheritance, knowing what is written in the will in advance eliminates some anxiety from an already stressful situation. If you add unequal inheritances among the kids, however justified or anticipated, to a first-time revealing of the will, you will unleash a tsunami of emotions. This can largely be avoided through successful conversations in advance.

In my opinion, and in my experience, it is best to treat your children equally in your will. If you want to treat them differently when they are alive, that is a different story. Of course, if one of your children is incapacitated in some way or has special needs, such as autism, that mean that he will not be able to care for himself, more financial assistance can be provided through either a special needs trust,[1] an insurance policy, or a larger portion of the estate. If this is the case, I recommend that everyone in the family know about it beforehand, so that there are no surprises. Failure to discuss it could set off feelings of anger and resentment in the other children. Even more potentially destructive, the parents will no longer be around to serve as targets on which the other kids can vent their anger. Situations like that often spiral into an unimaginable morass of conflict, resulting in a contesting of the will or ill feelings that last for generations.

If the parents explain to all the kids in advance why one offspring will be given a larger share, and if the will says, "I love you just as much, but this is what we felt we had to do as parents," it is possible that "bad feelings" and a will contest will not result. If hard issues are discussed in advance and children are prepared, family finances and relationships can remain unscathed during and after the estate transfer.

I have often seen families that limit the conversation to the tax issues because it is easier and safer. Very few families are comfortable having complete conversations about the family money. Being able to successfully and comfortably talk about family money really does take skills that not all of us possess. But they are skills you can learn, as you will see in Chapters 8 and 9.

There is another benefit to advance disclosure of what your children can expect to receive from your estate. Your adult children have their own financial planning to do. With the information you give them, they can adjust their expectations accordingly. Without cold, hard facts, most people will have a distorted assumption of how much they will inherit. Your children could be surprised by receiving either less than they expected or more than they imagined.

In my experience, affluent families have one of two distinct philosophies about money. There are those who believe that you should let the kids know about the family money. With good advisors and a sound estate plan, the successful family leaders look for targeted and scheduled opportunities to communicate with their heirs and begin to transfer their wealth based on a carefully constructed plan. Gifting monies outright and transferring assets through a trust or another type of entity, such as a family limited liability corporation or a family limited partnership, are some of the most popular strategies. On the other hand, there are families who do not want their kids to know the details about their money and avoid the subject. This strategy, typically found among the wealthiest segment of society, is based on the belief that money corrupts and limits ambition. These families want to keep knowledge of the family assets from the kids as long as possible.

Obviously, communication is dramatically different in the two groups. I do not agree with the families that choose not to discuss money in any way, with or without the assistance of an advisor. There is no guidance I can offer them. For those who accept the benefits of telling the kids about the family wealth, I have some suggestions. Whom and what you will tell should be guided in part by the family values (which we will discuss a little later in the chapter), and in part by each child's individual ability to handle the information. In many families, there is one child who has special issues involving money. This could be the result of bad habits, or maybe a physical, mental, or emotional challenge. If this is the case, you might need to have a separate conversation and create a special arrangement that will work for that person and her special circumstances.

However, in general, I think a balanced approach to sharing information about the family wealth and any special arrangements for members is the best option. You will still need to take into account each child's individual readiness and maturity. Obviously, the content and nature of the talk will change over time as the kids mature and demonstrate responsible behavior, and as the parents age and feel the need to share more information. However, whenever you approach the process, it is best to keep it simple. One idea to help with the communication is to have your attorney draft a simple summary that can be understood by a nonprofessional and distribute it to your heirs. Then, you might hold a family meeting to review the summary and answer any questions. Of course, family dynamics can interfere with this type of meeting. Some families may be concerned about protecting assets because they are worried about a potential divorce, or they may not trust their in-laws to use the information wisely. In general, however, it is best to at least tell all family members where the important financial documents are located, what to expect in the will, and what roles the heirs might play in the future, well in advance of any wealth transfer taking place.

I believe that the sooner you have the first of these conversations, the better. I understand that it is hard for, say, a seven-year-old to grasp the idea of family wealth. In that case, the use of an allowance can be a great opportunity to transmit family values and have meaningful conversations about money. Many of us grew up with an allowance. It was our first experience with understanding what money can buy. Allowances can set the stage for discussing how to be responsible for earning money and the various healthy ways to distribute it—spend, save, and share. When planning your children's allowances, think back to how your own parents handled the issue and whether or not you would like to repeat the experience, advise Eileen and Jon Gallo in their book, *Silver Spoon Kids*. They identify two basic rules about an allowance. First, all children should receive an allowance as an incentive to be involved in the family, to learn budgeting, and to learn about the consequences of their actions. And second, the appropriate amount of the allowance is whatever *you* feel is appropriate. The discussion should be focused on what the kids need to do to get their allowance, how the amount is determined, what it should cover, when and how it can be renegotiated, and how much control you retain over how it is spent. As for when, right around six years old, or first grade, is a good time to start.

One of the most important lessons you need to impart through an allowance is the value of delaying gratification. Research studies document the importance of delayed gratification in a child's early development. The marshmallow experiment is a famous test that Walter Mischel at Stanford University conducted in the 1960s. A group of four-year-olds were each given a marshmallow. They were told that if they could wait 20 minutes before eating the marshmallow, they would be given another. The researchers tracked the kids in the study for several years after the experiment and found that the kids who were able to go 20 minutes without eating the marshmallow were better adjusted and more dependable. They also scored 210 points higher on the Scholastic Aptitude Test. Being able to delay gratification translated into being able to save for another day, and that proved to be a very valuable life skill.

What are the best strategies to use to raise financially responsible children and transmit healthy values after they outgrow an allowance? As children grow into adulthood, they usually learn by example, watching how their parents acquire, use, and manage monies, whether or not their approach is healthy and balanced. Some parents think they should let their kids make their own money mistakes, either through an investment or through a job gone wrong. They feel that they should let them live on their own, then give them more control over their money after they have found success in a career that gives them a sense of personal accomplishment. I do not disagree with this approach. I have found that kids who are educated and independent, who have developed their own personal sense of self, and who have had some life experience tend to deal better with the family wealth. Life experiences can work wonders in providing lessons that help children learn the value of money and how to manage it. I think it makes sense to allow your young adult children to make early financial mistakes on their own—within reason, of course.

But prior to letting them fall down, you want to impart some lessons while they are still safely under your roof. Beginning in grade school, encourage your kids to work for rewards, whether by paying them for extra chores or by their babysitting or otherwise working outside the home. My son Eliot and a friend provided snow removal services to suburban type-A people who were not willing to wait for an established snowplow contractor to get to their driveway, or who did not want to pay a contractor's seasonal prices. In the summer, lemonade stands still pop up in my neighborhood. I am always impressed by how children can create a simple method for earning money. Some children will be interested in working in the local animal shelter for free, while others who are more material in nature might find a part-time job in a local retail store.

Working in the family company from the ground up and seeing the business from various different angles is another way you can help your child develop a sound work ethic and money values. Many professionals recommend setting up a family foundation or encouraging involvement in a specific charitable organization. This allows the family members to get acquainted with the financial details, such as the balance sheet, the cash flow (regular flow of income and expenses), specific investment instruments, the purpose of the entity, and evaluating nonprofits for donation or investment. It is always a good idea to let each family member take on a very specific role.

You might also consider setting up a family business or investment entity, such as a limited liability corporation or a family limited partnership, and giving each child a share. This exercise gives the kids insight into the business world. They can learn firsthand about asset classes, sound investment strategies, and how to evaluate business opportunities. The family meeting is a great vehicle for talking about the family values, creating a family mission statement, and beginning to share information about the family wealth.

It is a good venue for chatting about the foundation or shared business entity, and also about other assets and certain legal documents. The family meeting is also a great arena for young members to present an idea or issue they find compelling. You might even give them a chance to run a meeting. All of these will give you an opportunity to assess their individual readiness to take on more responsibility for the family money in the future.

Of course you cannot overlook the importance of trusted and competent advisors—accountant, attorney, and financial advisor—and an "Uncle Frank" or "Aunt Sally" figure, as David Darst suggests in his book *The Little Book That Saves Your Assets*, who is present to help run the meeting and hopefully make sure that there is an atmosphere of tolerance, patience, and impartiality. In addition, advisors can help the family leader communicate difficult subject matter that needs to be addressed, either one-on-one or as a group. Whomever you choose, it should be someone who has experience and expertise in counseling, in raising fiscally responsible kids, and in disclosing financial information and helping to prepare heirs.

Avi and Rebecca Greenberg were both born in Israel to parents who had emigrated from Europe after World War II. Avi's engineering studies were twice interrupted by combat, first in 1967 and then again in 1973. In 1978, the Greenbergs and their two children moved to the United States so that Avi could pursue his doctorate at a prestigious university. Never materialistic, but always driven, Avi found his life altered by combat. Having seen death firsthand, he committed himself to trying to do something to preserve life. He and Rebecca started a business designing and building medical devices. Avi was the scientist, and Rebecca was the businessperson. The Greenbergs had close and loving relationships with their two children, Rose and Charles. Rose, a veterinarian, was happily married with five children and lived in a nearby city. Charles lived with his gay partner and their one child in New York City.

From the time Rose and Charles were young, Avi and Rebecca wanted them to learn about the family business. The kids worked at the firm during summers and vacations. While Rose had always enjoyed her time working at her parents' company, her real passion was animals. She worked at a local animal shelter and dreamed of becoming a veterinarian. Her animal doctor dreams outweighed any real interest in the family business. After college, Charles worked for several years at a prominent Wall Street investment firm. He then launched his own small investment company. Like Rose, he did not have much interest in his parents' technology firm.

Charles and Rose preferred doing their own thing and being independent of family "control." The two kids enthusiastically attended all the family meetings that the family attorney ran, but they were not particularly engaged in the family money decisions. For the most part, they had no idea of the size of their parents' estate. Avi and Rebecca were perplexed. They wondered how to get their kids engaged in learning about the family investments, most of which were health sciences–related. Their goal was to make sure that Rose and Charles had the knowledge they needed to manage the portfolio or to select competent people to do so on their behalf.

To that end, at the recommendation of their financial advisor, Avi and Rebecca established a family foundation. This allowed the children to develop the charitable side of their personalities. It also exposed them to the administrative and investment decisions required to manage a portfolio of liquid securities and illiquid income-producing real estate. Avi and Rebecca had done a good job of giving the children incentives, but what continued to motivate Charles and Rose was their desire to avoid the powerful influence of their parents and the control of the trust and the trustees. As part of the estate plan, a family limited liability corporation was created to manage the family investments. All the family members were participants, each with different ownership interests. In addition, Avi and Rebecca funded two generation-skipping trusts,[2] with the full $5 million exemption available at that time, for each of the children's families, a part of which was used to purchase life insurance. The grandchildren received a percentage interest in the trust associated with their respective parent.

Unfortunately, conflict ensued between the siblings and the parents because of the big difference in the number of children that each adult child had in his or her family. Charles had only one child and felt that he was not being treated fairly by the gifting program, which was based on $13,000 per grandchild. To even out the inheritance, he wanted to take distributions for his personal benefit. Clearly, the parents' objective of trying to save on taxes was not compatible with protecting family relationships. However, the effort aimed at creating hardworking, independent, and non-materialistic children had succeeded.

So what is the lesson here? You can do all the right things all along the way to raise productive kids with good values and a charitable mindset in hopes of preparing them effectively to be your heirs apparent. But all that time and expense in planning is wasted if you create an estate plan that they consider unfair or unequal. Although it may be sound from an estate- and tax-planning point of view, the perceived inequality can create serious conflicts and have unintended consequences.

In my experience, people tend to act out when a family patriarch or matriarch dies. Just as a light switch turns off the light quickly, the family dynamic changes the moment a person is gone. If the heirs are treated differently in the will for no clear reason, then the negative impact can reverberate for generations. In Chapter 1, I gave an example in which a couple of children were disinherited or treated unequally. As you may recall, that mistake resulted in serious destructive anger and conflict that was passed on to the next generation of cousins. The family members now have nothing to do with one another. An estate plan is an expression of more than just money. Whether we like it or not, it sends a message. It is often taken as a token of parents' love for their children. It is seen as saying either "I love you" or "I do not love you." And a message delivered in a will is as permanent as death.

Avi and Rebecca should have had an open discussion with their kids before the trusts were created. They needed to talk about the disparity of beneficiaries and the impact of how that would play out between Rose and Charles. If they had talked about it and brought in advisors, they would have learned that there was an easy fix. The estate-planning attorney could have designed a flexible trust[3] so that Charles, who has only one child, could access the trust assets for his own personal use while he was alive. If Charles had been given a chance to discuss his concerns openly, then his parents might have known, in advance, that they should create a more flexible trust and therefore would have had their son on board with the tax-saving estate structure.

Avi and Rebecca also needed to discuss the inclusion of flexibility in both the trusts and the choice of trustees. Quite often, wealthy families use flexible trusts with generation-skipping provisions, established in jurisdictions that have eliminated or substantially modified a technical rule of law called the rule against perpetuities, that thus can continue for an extremely long time— essentially forever. The popularity of these trusts is understandable. They can prevent estates from being taxed upon the death of each generation and can last for generations. When they are properly drafted, these trusts can also protect individuals in the event of a divorce or death.

Flexibility can also be incorporated into these documents with regard to the issue of control. Trustees can give the beneficiaries, who in this case would be Rose and Charles, the opportunity to manage a portion of the monies and to receive funds for career opportunities or based on incentive clauses tied to goals, such as starting a business or earning a certain amount of money. What I recommend is the matching plan: a dollar-for-dollar match based on each dollar earned. The ultra-wealthy like to create discretionary trusts in jurisdictions with disclosure rules that are different. We have all heard of offshore trusts.[4] One of the reasons these families establish these trusts is to create a further layer of nondisclosure for their family members.

Having the right mix and type of trustees is critical when you are establishing these arrangements and communicating them to your children. When you are selecting third-party trustees, you need to consider someone who can serve as a surrogate parent— who shares your values, knows your children, and will make decisions as you would. A trustee can be a family member, a trusted advisor, or an institution, in various combinations. Often a trusted advisor, either an accountant or an attorney, will be asked to serve in combination with a family member. The flexible trusts I discussed earlier also allow for a change in trustees. In this case, the kids understand that they can change the trustee if they believe that the person their parents chose is not a good fit. It also helps the kids overcome the issue of "excess control" of the trust assets by either an individual trustee, a family attorney, or an institution. It is important to note that giving children such a power is not always a good idea and is, in some respects, inconsistent with one of the reasons people use trusts.

Most couples, like Avi and Rebecca, wonder when is the right time to create an estate plan. In my experience, doing so is typically driven by a life event, such as when your first child is born. Suddenly, when you look at your helpless new bundle of joy, you see the wisdom of creating a plan to care for her in case something happens to you. But as we know, life is not static, but rather is full of ever-changing transitions. As a result, your will and your estate plan need to reflect the changes in your life. That means that if you have another child, experience a divorce, remarry, sell a business, or lose a spouse, your will and your estate plan need to be updated. My hope is that you have an advisor who is encouraging or reminding you that it is time to revise and update your plan.

An estate plan, however, is only as good as what is included in it. If you do not document all your assets, then it is impossible for you to pass them to your heirs. That means that you need to make sure that all your assets and liabilities are revealed. Most attorneys and financial advisors have a questionnaire that can help you fully document your assets.

One final point: one of the most contentious aspects of settling an estate is the distribution of the personal property. Who gets mom's diamond engagement ring or her twenty-fifth-anniversary infinity diamond band? What about dad's collection of abstract expressionist artwork, or great-grandma's gold-plated china? These are often the biggest issues that surface when a family leader or spouse dies. And this is just as true for personal property that has little more than sentimental value.

There are as many ways to handle the distribution of the family heirlooms as there are families, and they differ in terms of the degree of conflict that can arise. I know one widower with three daughters who took his deceased wife's diamond pieces and got them all appraised. He then made three piles of equally valued diamond pieces. So while each daughter got diamonds with the same monetary value, the pieces of jewelry differed. One daughter got a diamond-encrusted watch, a tennis bracelet, and diamond studs. Another one got a diamond necklace and an engagement ring. And the third daughter got a single extraordinary ring. Of course, you cannot please everyone all the time. One of the daughters did not like any of the baubles she got. And two of the three daughters spent years stewing about their distributions.

An alternative, which may be perceived as more fair by the beneficiaries, is stating in the will that each child will get a substantially equal share, as long as they can agree. If they are unable to agree, then the executor will decide. Another clever way to distribute the goodies is to state in the will that each person picks something in a round-robin approach. The child that picks first in the first round picks last in the next round, and on and on until all the possessions have been disbursed. If the value is different at the end between the children, then a makeup provision in cash can be specified in the will.

The strategy that I prefer and that I recommend to my clients is to have a meeting with the children before you die. Give each child a chance to talk about his favorite items and come to a resolution on how everything is going to be divided in advance. You can also attach a letter to the will that reflects the agreement that was decided upon for the distribution of personal items at death. Having this conversation about personal items in advance also gives the family a chance to have a bigger conversation about the estate plan. Not only does it allow family members to share stories and talk openly about items that may have sentimental value, but it also encourages a healthy dialogue and cooperative spirit regarding estate matters. This could prove to be extremely valuable down the road.

Regardless of what approach you take in distributing the family tangible assets, make sure that they are securely and safely stored and/or properly insured under a home ownership policy or separate rider. Check the policy on a regular basis to make sure you are adequately covered for the current value of the items. Too often, these items are held for years without having insurance coverage as protection, or the policy is not updated for its rising value, then these precious and sentimental pieces are either lost or stolen and the family is left stunned and emotionally distraught for years.

On the subject of preparing heirs, instilling messages while your children are young, and then nurturing them by example and repetition, can help enforce desirable behaviors into adulthood. As the sign on President Harry Truman's desk said, "The buck stops here." You are ultimately responsible for creating healthy family intergenerational patterns and ensuring successful money transfers.

Developing and Communicating a Plan to Transfer a Family Business

Having a healthy intergenerational money transfer plan is even more important when a business is part of the transfer. That is because only 30 percent of family businesses survive into the second generation, only 12 percent survive into a third generation, and only a paltry 3 percent make it into a fourth generation or beyond, according to the Family Business Institute. Research indicates that this is largely because of a lack of proper succession planning. At one time, there was no need for succession planning: primogeniture ruled, and businesses went directly from the father to the oldest son. But succession determined by birth order was not always in the best interest of the company or the family members.

Today, with primogeniture no longer the standard, succession planning is a complicated task, and, as you can see from the statistics I just cited, few business owners appear to take it as seriously as they should. If families took as much effort to plan for their company's succession as they did in building the business, more companies would probably survive for multiple generations. Part of what makes a family business transfer so challenging is that the founder often sees the future of the business as being inseparable from the future of the family. The family business may be seen as the glue that keeps everyone together. However, the challenge is that both the family and the business must constantly be redefined, and their relationship reexamined, as family members grow and the business evolves.

To help guide them, families should consider hiring succession-planning specialists. After all, how many times can an individual business owner hand down a company to the next generation? There are accounting and consulting firms and psychologists who have that special expertise. These experts can help evaluate the readiness or ability of family members to take over a business. They can do informal testing, as well as do one-on-one interviews with family members, to provide feedback to the owner and help develop succession-planning goals. The process can uncover the degree of management skills, knowledge of the business, and emotional IQ of each family member or employee who might be considered a potential heir. A formal process using a specialized professional may not be necessary if the family's existing advisors, such as an accountant or attorney, are available to help evaluate the people and the succession options. Some family companies actually create their own board of advisors to help with these and other issues. Though this private company board of advisors may not have fiduciary[5] responsibilities the way a corporate board of directors does, it can be especially helpful during times of transition.

Regular family meetings are invaluable when it comes to determining who might be the right successor and when the transition should take place. A good place to start is to simply ask if anyone wants to actively participate in or one day inherit the family business. Often there is no child who is interested in the family business. In that case, a trusted and valued employee can be groomed for the position. Another possibility is that the company can seek an outside professional to serve as a bridge CEO until an interested grandchild is ready to take on the job and the ownership transfer can take place. Or maybe it is time to sell the business. The family and a trusted advisor or consultant can work through whatever equity participation issues arise. If one kid has the skillset and wants the business, and another is not interested, then the estate plan might give the child who is not receiving the business another asset to offset the difference in monetary value.

If a child has been involved in the business from an early age, the family leader may have been gifting the child a percentage of the business during her life, with the balance to come when the parent dies. In this case, the family should conduct meetings throughout the child's life to discuss how the business should be run, evaluate the different roles the child has assumed in the company, and see how the succession plan fits into the estate plan. In this way, the heir has the opportunity to make mistakes and learn from them. Family meetings can provide an opportunity to discuss the estate, tax matters, changes in management, and other issues at each point along the way, helping to prepare the heirs. If a family leader is having a difficult time disclosing details to the heirs, a trusted advisor can help to change his view over time.

Evaluating the situation and figuring out the succession plan is a multifaceted affair. As with an estate plan, the objective is to try to be fair and equal. Transferring ownership through gifting or selling requires open discussions that take into consideration the dynamics of the family as well as the tax issues. It is most important that the generation that is currently in control does not make decisions based solely on taxes. If the plan does not fit well with the family members, there could be irreparable damage to the family. It may require thinking like a prophet and trying to predict what the ramifications for both finances and family harmony will be. But it is essential if you want both the family and the business to survive.

Joe and Margaret Suarez owned a successful real estate company headquartered in a suburb of New York City. Joe is a second-generation Cuban American. Margaret's family members were also immigrants, but they came to New York from Ireland in the 1860s. Joe and Margaret met in high school. They married shortly after graduation. Joe went to work with his father, who had a small building-maintenance business, while Margaret went to nursing school. They had three children: a daughter, Katherine, and two sons, Carlos and Alex.

Joe Suarez built his father's small business into a very success-ful real estate services company, running office buildings in many of Long Island's expanding office parks. Margaret retired from nurs-ing in her early fifties, after a back injury, and found a role helping Joe with managing the business and overseeing family health issues that needed attention. Joe and Margaret dreamed of passing along the family business to their children and wanted to create a smooth succession plan. All the children were shareholders in the business, but Katherine was not actively involved. She was a family doctor in a small town about 20 miles from the rest of the family, and was passionate about her profession. The oldest son, Carlos, had stud-ied accounting and had been working in the family business since he graduated from college. His goal was to take over as the CEO—sooner rather than later. The other son, Alex, had an undergraduate degree in business and had worked outside the business in various management positions for a few years after he graduated. He even-tually decided to return to work in the family business.

Although Alex did not have the financial skills that Carlos had, he was better with people and had a higher emotional IQ. The employees and management valued and appreciated Alex. Joe and Margaret had always thought that Carlos would be the heir appar-ent, not least because he was the eldest. But after they saw how well Alex performed and how positively he was viewed, they decided to talk with their advisors about who would be the best choice. Eventually they decided that Alex should take over the business. The question then was how to distribute the stock and manage the personal and compensation issues.

Joe and Margaret, along with their advisors, spoke candidly with Carlos about his natural talent in the financial side of the busi-ness. He had just completed his MBA and would be a natural to assume the role of CFO. Fortunately, the current CFO was looking to retire in the next five years. A series of one-on-one meetings took place between the advisor, the accountant, the COO, the CFO, and each of the three children. The children would receive an equal number of shares in the family company. Compensation would be based on their job tasks. Alex, the CEO, would be compensated on a par with other CEOs in the industry, and Carlos would be compensated on a par with other industry CFOs. All the details and differences in pay, including perks, were discussed, and everyone was ultimately able to commit to the management changes. There would be an interim period of five years during which Joe would continue to serve as CEO and the current CFO would remain onboard while transferring the reins.

Even though she was not interested in the family business, Katherine was a little disappointed that she would no longer be on the company payroll, except for any annual profit distributions. To make up for that, her parents told her that for the next five years, they would gift her an amount equal to the compensation she had been receiving, and that she would receive her mom's jewelry over time. This plan was fully disclosed to her brothers, and they were on board completely.

I know I have covered a lot of ground in these chapters on transitions. I hope you were able to see your family in at least one of the transitions. If not, I hope I was at least able to convince you that you need to be aware of the financial impact of all of life's changes and the importance of the Money Talk as you navigate them. Gustav Mahler once said, "The real art of conducting consists in transitions." In the next chapter, I want to help you identify and understand the obstacles that may stand in the way of your conducting the greatest tool for dealing with difficult transitions: the Money Talk itself.

Things to Think About

- Transferring wealth from one generation to another requires teamwork among all family members and the family's chosen financial/investment advisor, trustees, and other fiduciaries. Have you put together your A-team of advisors, or do you need to make changes to the team?

(continued)

- Estate planning isn't just about transferring wealth; it's about transferring values as well. What are the values you want to transfer to the next generation? How will money affect the motivation and drive of the next generation? What impact, if any, will increased wealth have on their families, their lifestyles, and their communities?

- Parents often fail to discuss estate planning issues with their children due to fears that such talks will decrease motivation and drive or disappoint expectations. Children often avoid the topic because it means dealing with the inevitable deaths of parents. For a successful transition to take place, these fears must be overcome and the conversations need to take place.

- When designing your estate plan, it is best to treat children equally, particularly in a will. However, that does not mean that you need to treat them equally while you are alive. Have you treated your children differently? Have you thought about how to address that in your will?

- If, because of a special need, one child needs to be treated differently, it is important that everyone in the family understand this in advance and that the other children are aware of the "preferential" treatment.

- Distribution of personal property can be just as, if not more, contentious than distribution of financial assets. Consider obtaining appraisals and providing for equal value distribution in your will. Alternatively, a "round robin" approach might be stipulated. Advance discussion about wants and plans will reduce conflict.

- Advance disclosure of plans can help children make more prudent financial choices prior to any life transition. Do you believe your children are making financial choices based on anticipated wealth transfers?

(continued)

- Advance disclosure, informed discussions, and trusted advisors can help smooth family dynamics that often are strained when a patriarch or matriarch dies.
- An attorney may be able to draft a simple explanation of your estate plans that can serve as the basis for informed family discussions.
- If your children are young, have you used allowances as a learning tool? Have your children worked as volunteers, for pay, or in a family business? If they are old enough, have you considered giving them defined roles in a family business or a family investment entity?
- If a family business is to be transferred, look to hire business succession specialists who can not only help with the transition details, but who can assess the best roles for family members, based on their skills and wishes, and preserve family harmony as well as assets.
- Equal treatment of children in transferring a business need not necessarily mean equal ownership or equal future roles. Discrepancies can be addressed through special distributions or other means.
- As in transferring other assets, the successful transfer of a family business is best served by discussion and planning well before the transfer needs to take place and in concert with professionals.

8

Preparing the Inner Landscape

The Hidden Elements You Need to Consider Before and During the Money Talk

Errors, like straws, upon the surface flow;
He who would search for pearls must dive below.
—John Dryden

Every Money Talk is like a Shakespearean play. There is obvious drama and conflict on the surface, coming from the specific situations and circumstances. Then there are the hidden elements— the covert factors in life and the subtexts in the text—that make the conversations and the plays epic.

Having a Money Talk during one of the transitions I wrote about in the previous chapters—changes in financial circumstances, remarriage, retirement, aging parents, and transferring assets—is difficult enough because of the inherent drama in each situation. When you add in the hidden factors—issues of control and trust, the roles of family members, gender differences, basic neurological engineering, evolutionary behavior patterns, individual temperament and attitudes, age, family history, and culture—having a Money Talk appears to be a daunting challenge. That is why so many people avoid financial dialogues. But you can overcome the issues, conscious and unconscious, superficial and hidden, overt and covert. The first key is understanding the challenge. In this chapter, I will walk you through the 10 less obvious elements that threaten to turn your run-of-the-mill family drama into a tragedy of Shakespearean proportions: control, trust, family roles, gender differences, neurological engineering, evolutionary behavior patterns, individual temperaments, age, family history, and culture.

Does Anyone Really Have Control?

The *New Oxford American Dictionary* defines control as "the power to influence or direct people's behavior or the course of events."

Most people like to have control. Whether it is about a small matter, such as deciding where to make reservations for dinner Saturday night, or a larger issue, like who will be directing mom and dad's finances when they are unable to do so, the issue of control is always percolating under the surface in everyone's mind. Who is in control? Should that person have control? Is he the best person to exercise control? The common, unambiguous human drive for one person to control another can wreak havoc in all relationships and in every dialogue. But no issues better demonstrate the influences of control and power than those involving money.

The most useful question to ask about this issue is: does anyone really have control? Remarkably, the answer in most cases is no. Rarely does anyone truly have control over anything other than how she chooses to think, feel, and behave, says Dr. Charles Dwyer, professor at the University of Pennsylvania's Wharton School, former chairman of that school's Center for Applied Research, and director of its Management and Behavioral Science Center. The belief that we have control over any of the things around us, such as money or our family members, is just an illusion. Yet few people will acknowledge that.

This lack of acceptance is why, despite the illusory nature of control, the drive to exert it plays an integral part in conversations. Professor and author Deborah Tannen, in her book *I Only Say This Because I Love You*, writes that connection and control are the central forces that drive all conversations and relationships. She believes that there is an ongoing conflict between our need to be close enough to feel safe, but not so close that we feel suffocated. Tannen calls this the connection continuum. In addition, she believes that there is also an ongoing conflict between the desire to get the upper hand and get our needs met and the belief that no one should dominate someone else or tell someone else what to do. Tannen calls this the control continuum. A healthy Money Talk requires understanding and achieving closeness without being suffocating, and exerting power without being domineering. It also requires being one of the few who accept that, as Dr. Dwyer notes, no one really has control. This requirement was made clear when Dr. Dwyer and I discussed Kara Levin's situation on my radio show, *The M Word*.

Kara, the second oldest of four adult children, was frustrated because her older brother, Sam, took over all the conversations the siblings had about their parents' finances. Their parents, Heidi and Tom, both 85, still lived independently in their suburban New Jersey home. However, they were both failing fast.

The kids, Sam, Kara, Scott, and Doug, were all married professionals who lived in the Northeast. They began having weekly conference calls to discuss the steps they needed to take to manage their parents' daily and financial activities. These discussions centered on whether to move Heidi and Tom out of their home; if so, to where; if not, who would be hired to help; and how would this phase of their parents' lives be financed.

The problem, as Kara described it, was that as soon as the conference calls began, Sam abruptly demanded that he be in charge of what was discussed and who would be responsible for each item on the agenda. Sam, who at that time ran a trading desk at a large Wall Street firm, was used to directing people and events. He was also clearly knowledgeable about finances. Kara, a teacher, Scott, an engineer, and Doug, a web designer, all acknowledged that Sam was the logical person to manage the financial issues related to their parents' wealth. But they were offended by his controlling management style. The tension, anger, and resentment among the siblings escalated with every call. Making matters more complicated, Heidi and Tom were reluctant to turn over "control" of their daily physical care and finances to their children.

Even though Kara called her brother Sam a control freak, she and her siblings were really seeking more control of the situation and were frustrated because they felt they had so little. To extricate the family from an endless debate over "who is in charge," all four adult children needed to step back and think about their parents' needs first and what was best for them.

With that framework in mind, Dr. Dwyer suggested that Kara and her siblings each have separate conversations with their parents. During those solo meetings, the siblings could try to better understand what was causing their parents' fears and anxieties and what they wanted in the long run. When all these separate conversations had been completed, the entire family, including Heidi and Tom, could come together in person to discuss what the kids understood to be their parents' wishes.

This process would ensure that Sam would not dictate what needed to be done. He would be a participant in the conversation, not its director. It would also provide all the siblings with an individual chance to understand the decisions that needed to be made and what their parents wanted. Each could feel like a participant in a collective process. Ironically, I often find that surrendering some control to other family members or to an outside party, such as an accountant, attorney, or financial advisor, can help families overcome control issues that are sabotaging their Money Talks. I will describe the roles advisors can play in more depth in Chapter 9.

Trust Is Essential to Weather a Financial Crisis

While writing this book, I was struck by the tagline in an advertisement for a bank: "Remember when the word 'bank' didn't make you angry?" At first I was surprised by its boldness. Then I realized its brilliance. Ally Bank pointed out the elephant in the room: consumers, investors, and other stakeholders are having trouble trusting financial institutions after the financial crisis of 2008.

Financial services and banking remain the least trusted industries in the world, according to the 2012 Edelman Trust in U.S. Financial Services study. Just 46 percent of the respondents in that study said that they trust financial services, and only 41 percent trusted their banks. But that is a remarkable improvement over the previous year's study, in which only 25 percent said that they trusted their banks. Individuals need to trust that if they deposit their paychecks every two weeks, the money will be there when they need it. As Americans, they need to trust that the Federal Deposit Insurance Corporation will insure their deposits or, as members of a larger investment community, that they can access the funds they have invested long term with a global institution.

One of the guests on my radio show, Frank Luntz, a prolific author of books about communication strategies and public opinion and the founder of the Word Doctors, a message creation and image management firm, noted a significant shift in the public's perception of the future. We were once the most optimistic society, always believing that tomorrow would be better than today. For the first time since 1993, according to Luntz, we believe that our kids are going to have a lower quality of life than we do. A lot of this, he believes, has to do with a loss of trust in large institutions, such as banks, the government, and the media.

While the numbers remain troubling, trust in individuals and institutions in the financial services industry is slowly on the rise. According to research by Northstar, a respected financial research company, 74 percent of survey respondents trusted their primary financial advisor, up from 61 percent in 2009. And 66 percent of survey participants trusted their primary financial institution, up from 48 percent in 2009. Ethical business practices and listening to customer needs and feedback are the most important elements in building U.S. stakeholders' trust in financial services, according to the most recent Edelman Trust in U.S. Financial Services study. The prior year, the Edelman report cited honest communication and transparency as keys to reputation.

The Edelman report also said that participants believed that the most credible source of financial information was the broker, advisor, agent, or banker. What this implies is that investors' trust is tied to their personal experience with the professional who serves them. And, although I cannot cite specific research to back up my belief, I have always thought that investors whose work with an advisor is successful trust the advisor more than the institution. Giving financial advice is, I believe, about personal trust between individuals.

Even deeper than the level of trust needed between a financial advisor and a client is the level of trust that family members need to have in one another during a health crisis, during a marital conflict, or when facing end-of-life issues. In their book *Building Trust*, Robert Solomon and Dr. Fernando Flores cite three major components that must coexist within family relationship if trust is to be sustained: reliability, sincerity, and competence.

Reliability means that family members do what they say they are going to do. If a parent repeatedly says that he is going to show up at a soccer game and does not, then he is setting up a pattern of negative expectations and unreliability. The child receives the message that she is unimportant and that her parent cannot be relied upon. This pattern can also develop with other family members, such as spouses and siblings.

Sincerity means that an individual's "internal story" matches up with his "outer story." Is what the world sees different from what the individual feels inside? With insincerity come false promises, and those lead to an erosion of trust.

Competence means that the family member has the capability and capacity to accomplish the required task. You would not give a family member who is not the least bit interested in finances, or who has little aptitude for them, the task of determining the best estate-planning techniques or finding an advisor to work with the family.

Family Roles Are Played Out During Money Talks

Have you noticed that there is usually one adult child who takes on the responsibility of caring for aging parents? The choice could be based on geography: maybe this person is physically closest to mom and dad. The selection could also be based on time availability: perhaps two of the kids are working full time and another is single or has a flexible work situation. Or the decision could be based on temperament: it could be that one of the children is more patient and is comfortable working with people who are involved in sensitive situations.

Just because one individual naturally takes the lead in a particular situation does not mean that the others should not play a part. There are as many roles for various family members to play as there are family members. Finding the right role for each individual depends on a myriad of characteristics, both internal and external.

In the Stern family, it was natural for the youngest son to come to the aid of his aging, widowed father. The father, Eugene, an avid skier and biker, was a successful entrepreneur who had made a great deal of money in textile manufacturing before he sold his company in the late 1990s.

Raised in a suburb of Charlotte, North Carolina, by their stay-at-home mom, Joan, Eugene's three sons, Eli, Spencer, and Adam, acquired a strong sense of family responsibility as well as professional ambition. Each son pursued graduate studies: Eli in law, Spencer in finance, and Adam in medicine. Eli and Spencer, each married with two children, lived in Atlanta and Cleveland, respectively. Adam, an emergency room doctor, was single and lived in Los Angeles.

When Joan died of lung cancer in the early 1990s, Eugene relocated to Santa Fe, New Mexico, where the family had a second home. Though many happily married widowers remarry soon after losing their wives, Eugene did not. He filled his life with skiing, biking, traveling, and managing his own investments. Frequent visits from his sons and lots of friends kept him busy. But when he was in his late seventies, his age caught up with him, and he had a series of five surgeries in 18 months. He needed family help.

Adam was the most caring and qualified of the three children. Fortunately for the family, he had the professional flexibility to care for Eugene during his surgeries. It soon became clear that Eugene needed to have family nearby, not just for his physical care, but also for help with financial management. Adam, who had always been interested in investing and had done well with the help of a good financial and investment advisor, moved from Los Angeles to Santa

Fe. He got a job at a local hospital and slowly began to take over the family finances.

Both Eli and Spencer, while quite capable of stepping in, didn't have Adam's financial aptitude, medical expertise, or his flexibility. They trusted Adam, who fit Solomon and Flores's definition: reliable, sincere, and competent. Within a year of moving to Santa Fe, Adam was given full power of attorney over Eugene's affairs with the full blessing of his brothers. He has quarterly conversations with Eli and Spencer about the family finances and Eugene's physical state. The conversations often include a financial advisor and an accountant. These trusted professionals help with any issues that may arise and help facilitate family communication on both personal and financial issues.

Accepting Inherent Gender Differences

Everyone knows that men and women are different. However, after more than 20 years working as an advisor, I have found that those differences are profound when it comes to money. Men and women make financial and investment decisions very differently. And no matter how much we try to "understand" each other, those differences can never be eradicated. That is because the differences are rooted in the physical structure of our brains.

Gender differences have been the subject of dozens of studies, with more than one million participants in 30 countries across the globe. Every single one of those studies confirmed the male-female differences. There were some nuanced cultural disparities that were found, but the results were remarkably consistent regardless of place of origin or language, according to Barbara Annis, coauthor of *Leadership and the Sexes: Using Gender Science to Create Success in Business*.

Consider the different traits we assign to men and women. These are much more than stereotypes. They are hardwired physical differences that affect thinking and behavior. Men and women have different-sized anterior cortex areas of the brain. As a result, women tend to think in a more weblike, contextual way, while men think in a more linear, focused manner. According to Annis, men generally select one or two sources of information and make a quick, independent decision. Women, on the other hand, generally take in information from multiple sources, weigh their options, and make collaborative decisions.

Think about your own experiences. I am sure you have found that women tend to ruminate and constantly rehash experiences and events, while men tend to act quickly and never look back. Men might ask, "What do you think?" when they are looking for an opinion or a decision to reach closure. Women, on the other hand, might view that question as an invitation for further discussion.

Brain science studies have also shown that how and what we remember and how we process words and emotions differs between the genders. According to Annis, women tend to absorb more information through their five senses than men do, and then store it for later use in conversations. Not surprisingly, women generally use more words than men, and women have stronger connections between memory, emotional centers, and communication. That makes it easier for them to retrieve events, bring up past conflicts, and discuss emotional issues.

I am sure that you can recall long conversations with one of the women in your life—whether a spouse, sibling, friend, or coworker—during which she raised emotion-laden issues and inserted facts from knowledge acquired long ago. Women need to process emotional events and personal problems by talking them over with others, often speaking to outsiders about family members. This is one of the fundamental ways in which women form friendships, says Deborah Tannen, the bestselling author of *I Only Say This Because I Love You*, among other books. Men, on the other hand, can view speaking to outsiders about family members as a betrayal. Tannen says they simply do not understand the purpose. Men base their friendships on sharing activities, not secrets. When it comes to resolving conflict, men prefer doing something physical, while women prefer to discuss the issues. It is easy to see how this gender difference can become a source of conflict.

Women and men also have different-sized prefrontal cortex areas of the brain. This affects short-term versus long-term thinking. In a study she made of decision making on Wall Street, Annis found that women in the boardroom focused on the longer-term impact of decisions, while men focused on the bottom line and short-term gains.

There's also a brain difference that may account for what people have historically referred to as "women's intuition." The area behind the prefrontal cortex, called the insular part of the brain, is larger in women than in men. It has been suggested that this could account for a woman's ability to pick up the mood of a group of people that may have nothing to do with observable facts.

Finally, the tendency to multitask or act sequentially can be traced to brain structure. There is a thick band of nerve fibers called the corpus callosum that lies between the left and right hemispheres of the brain. These nerve fibers are 24 percent wider in women than in men. As a result, men tend to take on tasks one at a time, while women tend to multitask.

These gender differences translate into men and women approaching money decisions differently. One of the most striking differences that becomes apparent early on is that women and men tend to have different goals. Men are typically more focused on the bottom line of an investment and less interested in the long-term goals of providing for the security of the family and the community. When asked, men generally say that funding their own retirement is their top priority. In contrast, women generally focus on the journey to get to the destination, and they want to make sure that their children are protected before they address retirement concerns. Women also see crises looming in the future, whereas men are looking at a shorter time horizon.

Men and women also tend to invest differently. Interestingly, female investors actually outperform male investors, according to Brad Barber and Terrance Odean, two professors from the University of California, Davis. In their groundbreaking 2001 article *Boys Will Be Boys: Gender, Overconfidence, and Common Stock Investment*, Barber and Odean found that men traded 45 percent more than women, resulting in net returns that were almost a full percentage point less than those of women. The study identified overconfidence as the cause of the problem.

A 2005 Merrill Lynch Investment Managers survey found that women make fewer investment mistakes than men, not because women are smarter, but because they are better at avoiding them. For example, men are more likely than women to allocate too much to one investment (32 percent versus 23 percent), trade securities too often (12 percent versus 5 percent), and buy a hot investment without doing any due diligence (24 percent versus 13 percent).

The survey also found that men were more likely to make the same mistake twice. Of the men who said that they bought a stock without doing any research, 63 percent of them said they did it again, compared with 47 percent of women who made that mistake. Of the women who reported that they waited too long to sell an investment, 50 percent repeated the mistake, as opposed to 61 percent of men. Finally, when asked about ignoring the tax consequences of an investment, a robust 68 percent of men reported doing it more than once, whereas only 47 percent of women were repeat offenders.

Men typically become more involved in saving and investing gradually, over the course of their lives, while women usually become involved as a result of a life event, such as the birth of a child, divorce, retirement, or a death.

Despite their investing as a result of life events, women are more consistent and hold their investments longer than men. And while they may be more proactive about initiating their savings and investments, men tend to be more active traders and aggressive investors. A 2010 study by Northwestern University's Kellogg School of Management found that higher levels of testosterone were associated with higher tolerances for risk taking. Women tend to be more conservative than men when choosing investment vehicles. They show more concern about preserving their money than men do.

So what does this mean? Basically, when you are talking about money, there will be an unavoidable, natural level of conflict between you and a family member of the opposite sex. And when that inevitable conflict arises, you will each respond to it differently. Men will get angry and want to argue and debate. Women will feel rejected and want to be acknowledged, understood, and validated.

Getting past these differences requires different tactics. Women need to give men space. Leave him alone. Do not press. Let him argue. This will help him get through his anger. Men need to listen, nod, and let women talk about the disagreement. Let her express herself freely without feeling judged or having to defend her thoughts and feelings. Acknowledge that these differences exist, and then try to stand in the other person's shoes. Even though you do not see the situation the same way, be sensitive to the other's point of view. Try to communicate your feelings about the particular situation, but be aware that your minds are not opposed, they are just different. As Barbara Annis put it, "great minds think unlike." Believe me, after years of guiding Money Talks, I have learned that both kinds of minds are needed in solving today's complex financial problems.

And, awareness of the differences is critical in achieving goals together and communicating openly with each other.

Joe and Michelle Allen, a well-to-do African-American couple, have been married for 10 years. Joe, who still resembles the high school football player he once was, is chief talent officer at a fast-growing software company. Michelle, a petite bundle of energy, is a partner in a politically connected law firm that specializes in environmental issues. They have two children, Joe Jr., age 5, and Carrie, age 8, who both attend a nearby private school. Because Joe and Michelle are both career-driven and have done very well financially, they employ a full-time nanny to take care of the children when they're not in school.

Joe prides himself on his knowledge of the markets and enjoys following financial news, but he has no formal training or real expertise in money management. He likes day trading and looks to avoid fees. Michelle is interested in making sure that Joe Jr. and Carrie's college accounts are fully funded and that the family's other monies are properly managed for the long term. She is eager to set a moderate strategic course with an advisor she trusts, while Joe wants to invest in a more independent, aggressive manner. The result of all these differences is that the Allens have argued about money for years without coming to a conclusion.

When the tension between them concerning investing issues resulted in a weekend of their not speaking to each other, Joe relented and agreed that they needed to bring in a neutral party. The CFO at Joe's company was already a client of mine and suggested that the Allens meet with me.

The war between them was obvious within a few minutes. I counseled them that they needed to listen to and be aware of each other's goals and differences in opinions. I gave each of them the opportunity to discuss his or her particular point of view and repeatedly stressed that each needed to understand the other's feelings before a common solution could be reached.

As the session progressed, Joe debated and argued to let off steam. Michelle vented by bringing up past events and expressing her emotional concerns in vivid detail. I nodded and pushed for patience so that each of them could fully communicate his or her feelings. By the end of the session, they each felt heard by the other and agreed to a second meeting with me. We were starting to make some progress.

At the second session, we acknowledged the differences of approach, objectives, and emotional and communication styles. I then explained the brain-based reasons for these conflicts and that these were universal traits. With that information, the Allens gained important insight and began not to blame each other. By the end of the second session, it all seemed to make complete sense to them. They felt relieved to understand the reasons for the seemingly irresolvable conflict they had been having. The Allens were finally able to openly discuss their wants and goals with each other. Together we forged a plan that allowed each of them to meet both individual needs and joint objectives without rancor or anger.

Joe and Michelle agreed to fund their children's accounts with a strategy based on their children's ages, using Section 529 plans[1] with a five-year gift front-loading option. This meant that they could each invest $60,000 for each child, based on a $12,000 annual gift tax exclusion for each without gift tax issues, while amortizing the gifts over five years. They assigned those monies to professional money managers with the idea of adding to them over time as part of a gifting program. They also agreed to establish an irrevocable trust for noneducational purposes that would use a portion of their generation-skipping tax and estate tax exemptions. They were able to agree on guardians and trustees.

At the same time, the Allens allocated a negotiated amount of Joe's earnings to a special account that he could invest as he chose. However, a proviso was that it had to be reviewed on a quarterly basis with a member of my team and annually with me for oversight of the risk, suitability, and performance of his investments. The Allens then agreed to assign a moderate risk profile to the bulk of the family's monies. This included retirement accounts that they both had with their employers and some inherited monies that Joe had from the death of his grandmother and Michelle had as part of a family trust over which she had some investment influence with her trustee. Ultimately, my team and I reviewed all the investments and reallocated them based on the new investment strategies. We assigned the monies (other than Joe's independent account) to institutional money managers and established a schedule for regular reviews.

With the conflict between them resolved and their plans in place, Joe and Michelle felt a sense of accomplishment and some much-needed peace of mind. Later, in a telephone conversation, Michelle confided to me that their overall relationship has benefited from learning how to interact in a gender-intelligent way. As I am writing this book, I have an upcoming appointment with them to tackle their insurance portfolio and look to incorporate it into their estate plan.

Brain Physiology Affects Money Choices

It is not only the differences between the male and female brains that make the Money Talk problematic; it is the way *all* of our brains work. There is an emerging field called neuroeconomics that combines neuroscience, psychology, and economics to examine how the functioning of the brain influences financial decision making.

Neuroscience has identified two different kinds of thinking that take place in our brains. The reflexive system is the part of the brain that governs our emotions, feelings, and instinctive responses. The reflective system is the analytic thinking part of the brain that allows us to access our rational side.

The reflexive system is located underneath the cerebral cortex in what are called the basal ganglia and limbic areas. These parts of the brain process stimuli and responses at such lightning speed that they may finish responding to an event long before the conscious part of your brain realizes that there was anything to respond to. Physical examples of this system are sweaty palms, shaky hands, dilated pupils, and tensed muscles. People who make financial decisions on an emotional basis in the heat of the moment are relying on their reflexive system. As a result, they act without thinking through their decisions.

The reflective system is centered in the prefrontal cortex behind your forehead. This is the part of the frontal lobe that wraps around the core of your brain. It is the area of the brain that is used to solve complex problems. It is the home of the uniquely human abilities to make long-term plans, weigh actions against possible consequences, and consider the pros and cons of a decision before making it. If the reflexive or emotional brain wants to act without conscious thought, the reflective or analytical brain wants to think . . . and think . . . and think. People who rely on the reflective system can never make a financial decision. I am sure you know people like that.

The secret to making good financial decisions is to use both systems in the brain and strike a balance between responding from pure instinct and taking time to think more carefully.

To encourage reflective thinking, it is best to create a plan when making financial and investment decisions. It is important that your plan be based on a specific set of financial and investment objectives that take into account your risk tolerance, time horizons, and liquidity requirements. The financial plan should tackle the basic short- and long-term goals of the family members—for example, your eventual retirement, your estate legacy, and the education of your grandchildren. My recommendation is that your plan be documented by either you, your advisors, or the institution with which you work. Financial institutions have financial planning software and prototype investment policy statements to help guide families in creating a personalized plan and/or investment policy. Financial advisors such as I regularly work with clients to determine their goals and dreams and the proper strategies, both short and long term, to help them achieve those goals and dreams. An investment strategy addresses the various asset classes and instruments that can be included, as well as those that are restricted. And it will usually outline the benchmarks to be used to measure performance and determine the amount of risk that can be taken. It will further serve as directions for the person's advisors and money managers.

Most important, having a thoughtful plan in place and following it can help you stay the course during times of market tumult when your reflexive brain is pushing you to make sudden and often poor choices for yourself and your family.

Of course, there are times when the reflexive brain is alerting you to important dangers. What if you had had a hunch about Lehman Brothers the week before it went under, or about Enron before the company fell apart and became worthless? Relying on your instincts and selling then would have been a great move. Few people have such prescient insights, but they do exist. Malcolm Gladwell's bestseller *Blink* describes how the subconscious can sometimes allow us to make correct decisions with remarkable speed, in what seems to be reflexive thinking. And women, as we have discussed, have the advantage of superior intuition because of the insular area behind the prefrontal cortex section of the brain.

During times of crisis, such as the Great Recession of 2008, fear typically overwhelms individuals as events unfold. If the reflective system is not tapped, people's judgment can be compromised and mistakes can result. During those tumultuous days, financial advisors like me were constantly talking on the telephone with and meeting with clients. Our goal was to encourage them to embrace the reflective part of the brain, rather than selling out at the bottom of the market and incurring real losses, not just paper ones based on the current conditions. Their already having a plan in place was critical to that end. Those who stuck to their plans and were able to hang on reaped the benefits as the markets rebounded.

According to research, individuals tend to react emotionally to economic events, whether positive or negative. As a result, many people get into the market when they should be exiting or rebalancing, and exit the market when they should be staying the course or entering. Consequently, their long-term returns suffer and do not even keep up with inflation. Typically, when the markets experience a large economic event and hit bottom, they will rebound significantly within six months to a year. Obviously, there are times when people should follow their gut defensive instincts, particularly if not doing so would lead to months of sleepless nights and severe stress. However, such reflexive actions should be tempered with reflective thinking and discussions with financial advisors, portfolio managers, and family members before taking thoughtless action.

Mitchell Green, a successful 48-year-old public relations executive, is married to Rachel, a 47-year-old financial analyst at a small boutique Wall Street firm. Mitchell and Rachel, who always look as if they have just stepped out of a Ralph Lauren ad, have been married for 14 years. They have managed their own retirement accounts as well as other monies that they hold separately in mutual funds, exchange-traded funds, and other investment vehicles.

Rachel knew her risk tolerance and created a well-diversified portfolio reflecting a moderate and balanced investment strategy that she could maintain despite the roiling of the markets. Mitchell, on the other hand, had never assessed his risk tolerance or evaluated the risk associated with the investment choices he made. Like so many investors, Mitchell had not created an investment plan that took into account how much of a portfolio loss he could endure when the markets declined precipitously. He lost half the value of his portfolio during the sudden market downturn beginning in 2000. He recouped that value and more during the bull market years through 2007. But when the financial crisis hit in 2008, Mitchell watched his portfolio slide further and further.

Mitchell shared his fears with Rachel, who urged him to just hang on, because the market would eventually rebound. By the beginning of March 2009, however, with his portfolio down more than 50 percent from its high before the crisis, Mitchell could not take it anymore. He sold every penny of his stock portfolio and parked the money in cash. He sold out three days before the official bottom of the market and didn't reinvest the money in equities until November 2009. By then, the market had climbed significantly from its low. Instead of buying low and selling high, Mitchell sold low and bought high.

Because Rachel had assessed her tolerance for risk, felt comfortable with her asset allocation and investment plan, and had a long-term strategy in place, she was equipped to stay the course. Though the value of her portfolio fell, it didn't decrease as much as the equity markets because she held several different asset classes, including Treasuries and tax-free securities, which actually posted positive results through the crisis.

Why had Mitchell and Rachel reacted so differently?

First, although Mitchell had been understandably thrilled when he doubled his portfolio during the bull market, unlike Rachel, he had never answered the essential questions: how much risk are you comfortable taking; how much volatility is inherent in your portfolio; and how far are you willing to see your investments fall? Mitchell should have taken the time to think and learn about market cycles and investor behavior and to examine past bear markets. Then he could have created an investment strategy or policy and actually put it in writing in some form, tapping into the reflective side of his brain. Had Mitchell assessed his risk temperature, had a plan that reflected it, and then stuck to it, he probably would not have sold at the bottom.

Second, Mitchell was not able to control a powerful neurological instinct: the fear that he would lose all his money if he continued to stay invested in the stock market. Jason Zweig, a columnist for the *Wall Street Journal* and author of *Your Money and Your Brain: How the New Science of Neuroeconomics Can Help Make You Rich*, urges people in that situation to try their best to stop thinking and obsessing about their portfolio, and instead track their feelings in a diary. Writing about the desire to sell everything, instead of doing it, can help you keep your emotions in check. I have found that in addition to writing down concerns, just talking about the fears and the potential risks can help families cope with financial and investment issues that are not even related to frightening market cycles.

For instance, there are times when I have suggested that families who are in denial about the health of an aging parent and do not want to face the potential crisis that is looming have a durable power of attorney and designate a trusted member of the family as agent in the event of the parent's disability. This decision is usually made in the context of a larger plan to transfer wealth from one generation to the next. I have also counseled the family member who has been chosen as the overseer that while positive thinking is useful, extreme optimism and overconfidence in her own capabilities can be dangerous. Every family member involved needs to balance his thinking and help the rest of the family to balance theirs as well. I tell the family members that there is no shame in saying, "I do not know," and remind them that reaching out for help from professionals can be essential.

I wish I could have convinced Mary Prentice to do that sooner. Mary was not willing to ask for help after her husband of 55 years died and her own cognition began to decline. A dignified and stoic 82-year-old who never appeared ruffled, she tackled the job of working through the paperwork and details involved in executing the estate plan that her husband had meticulously and intelligently prepared with his advisors. Mary initially had an enormous amount of help from her son-in-law, Charles, who was a successful corporate lawyer. However, because he was so busy with his practice and was dealing with an autistic son, he was not able to commit the time and attention that Mary needed. He also didn't notice the changes that were taking place in her cognitive abilities. Although she was able to work with the attorney and successfully settle the estate, within a few months, she began to leave bills unpaid, forget appointments, and fail to follow through with the daily tasks of life. It was not until her daughter, Emily, visited from out of town and spent several days of concentrated time with Mary that the family became aware of the cognitive changes. When Emily and Charles together confronted Mary about her inability to take care of herself, her reflexive thinking kicked in, and she reacted emotionally and belligerently. That Money Talk did not go well.

However, Emily and Charles were able to reflect on their actions and the unfortunate outcome and decided to take a different approach. They enlisted the help of professionals, including Mary's gerontologist and a trained social worker from the local family service agency. Together they helped Mary tap into more productive reflective thinking. With their support, Mary was able to recognize that she was no longer at the top of her game. She accepted that she had to allow others to start taking control of her personal and financial life. Mary agreed to let Emily and Charles serve as her power of attorney agents and as cotrustees of her trust, and thereby take control of her bill paying, her physical care, and the management of her financial assets.

At the same time, Emily and Charles recognized that they did not have the skills or the time to oversee Mary's financial and investment affairs. They needed to find someone who was capable and trustworthy to serve as the family financial advisor. This became apparent when Emily and Charles discovered that a longtime family friend who was a stockbroker had been placing Mary in unsuitable investments, "churning" the account to generate commission dollars rather than serving the client. With the support of her children, her lawyer, and her accountant, Mary hired me to help her create a financial plan and an investment strategy for the family and place the monies with professional money managers. My team and I were also able to create a structured and repeatable process to guide all the financial decisions going forward. As you can imagine, the plan included frequent Money Talks with and among family members.

Breaking Free of Instinctive Behavior Patterns

Beyond the gender-specific structures of our brains and the different ways of thinking that take place inside those brains, we all have primitive behavior patterns that can turn Money Talks into Money Fights.

Evolutionary psychology is an emerging field parallel to neuroeconomics. Evolutionary psychologists believe that much of our behavior has evolved from the adaptations that our ancient ancestors made in order to survive in their primitive world. They suggest that, for example, how we react to a stock market crash is linked to how our ancestors reacted to seeing a saber-toothed tiger. They believe that humans have evolved further than other animals not because we have fewer instinctive behaviors than those animals, but because we have more. They suggest that in losing touch with our instincts, we get in the way of our own success. Reconnect with your instincts, the evolutionary psychologists urge, and you will enhance every aspect of your life. While I am not able to attest to the curative powers of reconnecting with our primitive instincts, I can vouch that being aware of them helps us improve financial communication.

Dr. Hendrie Weisinger, a clinical/organizational psychologist and author of *The Genius of Instinct: Reclaim Mother Nature's Tools for Enhancing Your Health, Happiness, Family and Work*, has identified six instinctual tools that can either lead to problems or help us solve problems. Shelter-seeking instincts can motivate you to find an empowering environment, relationship, or job. Care-soliciting instincts can drive you to protect your vulnerabilities. Caregiving instincts can help you develop and nurture people for the future. Beauty instincts can influence you to make yourself desirable to others. Cooperative instincts can help you galvanize people to work together. And curiosity instincts can encourage you to stay ahead of the pack.

How do our primitive instincts influence our financial and investment decisions? When one person sells during a market downturn, many follow. This is in part connected to the instinct to seek cooperation. To be effective in the financial markets today, you need to be an independent thinker. But 25,000 years ago, independent thinking would have resulted in your being ostracized and potentially thrown out of the cave.

In addition, the instinct to seek shelter is connected to the fear of loss that is central to the way investors behave. You may hang on to an inappropriate and money-losing investment, just as an individual 25,000 years ago hoarded water because he didn't know when he would find the next spring. I have found that many clients want to irrationally hold on to stocks that they inherited from a dear relative or earned at a company where they worked for years or that their family founded. They are attached to the investments emotionally and feel safe and secure simply because they own them. Other investors do not feel comfortable unless they have an overly large amount of cash on the sidelines. They see cash as the ultimate security, and they never think they have enough of it. They decide to sell an investment and convert it to cash in a volatile market because holding it challenges their need for safety and certainty.

Of course, there was no money in prehistoric times. But there was a medium of human interaction and exchange that played a similar role back then: sex. Thousands of years ago, prehistoric men were the hunters and women were the childbearers and gatherers. Sex was used as a form of exchange: women offered it in exchange for food, and men used their success as hunters to entice women into sex. As a result, sex became associated with manipulation and survival. It also became associated with a fair amount of shame and discontent. Today, money is our source of survival. We need it to obtain the basic requirements for surviving and flourishing. And the lack of it is also associated with all kinds of emotions, including fear, anger, and lack of self-esteem. Because of the evolutionary and deep-seated connections between money and sex, conversations about money and about sex are unconsciously linked and equally uncomfortable.

You cannot change the uncomfortable and instinctual connection between money and sex—it's the result of thousands of years of evolution, and it is deeply rooted in our DNA. But you can draw upon an understanding and awareness of all the basic instincts that are in play and respond to them in a positive way.

When you are about to have the Money Talk with a family member, it is essential that you make sure that he feels secure and comfortable before, during, and after the talk. That is why many successful financial advisors go out of their way, when communicating with clients, to make them feel comfortable. They institute strategies and use certain selected words to facilitate a feeling of safety in their clients. To have a successful Money Talk with your family members, whether the advisor is present or not, it is important that they perceive the environment as safe. Create a meeting space that is attractive and calming. Offer them something to drink. Speak in a gentle tone, and use words such as *safety*, *security*, and *protection*. And let the family members know that the information discussed will remain confidential unless they choose otherwise.

A big mistake that people make in their Money Talks with family members is to give the impression that the conversation is a threat or a ploy to take control. Because of the hardwired connection between money and sex, women feel particularly threatened by any gesture that they perceive as an attempt to manipulate them. Perhaps you are setting a budget for an elderly female relative or having a conversation with her about a power of attorney. In that discussion, your relative might feel threatened because she perceives that something will be taken away from her. Just imagine the conflict that could ensue.

Another instinct is cooperation. To encourage a spirit of cooperation, let family members know that you want everyone to work together to achieve the agreed-upon goal. If mom or dad is in need of a new housing situation, someone to handle the finances, and someone to provide physical care, one strategy might be to give each child a role in dealing with the issues so that everyone feels that she is contributing, no one feels left out, and no one feels that she is taking on all of the burden.

A family leader who has accumulated wealth and is interested in helping to prepare her heirs to successfully manage the monies they inherit could also tap into the cooperative instinct. She could decide to have regular family meetings and give each child a role in these meetings. One child might research a nonprofit to receive a contribution from the family charitable trust or foundation. Another child could lead a meeting about grandma's deteriorating health and the need to review her messy finances. If all family members are included in regular meetings and are working together to identify and sort out issues, a spirit of cooperation takes hold.

As a financial advisor, I let my clients know that I am just part of their team of financial advisors at Morgan Stanley, that I lead a wonderful staff of professionals who will work in concert to help them through life's transitions. This implies a further level of cooperation.

People instinctively seek beauty. If you are the family member who is chosen to lead a meeting or coordinate the event and lead the communication, make sure you are well dressed. There is a reason that professional advisors are always in formal business attire. If you want to be taken seriously when you are discussing a serious matter, you have to look like a serious and successful person. Would you feel more comfortable trusting your estate or investments to someone who shows up in a fashionable business suit or someone who shows up in jeans and a wrinkled T-shirt?

Individual Temperament and Attitudes Are Expressed Financially

We all know people whose first response to everything is negative or who stress out at the slightest change in a carefully scheduled day. We also are familiar with people who see the silver lining in the darkest cloud or who can roll with every curveball they're thrown, no matter how potentially traumatic. It seems as if some people are hardwired to be happy and to have a more upbeat nature, while others are born with a negative disposition. For years, people have thought that a person's temperament is a genetic predisposition that they can never change; they cannot fight their genes. But recently, psychologists have come to realize that people are capable of changing their temperament and attitude.

Happiness is actually a subjective experience, one that is internally driven by our own reality or our perception of reality. It is dependent on what your brain is deciding to focus upon. When your brain is scanning for all the negative and stressful events of the day, and all the hassles, it actually misses many of the positive attributes of life that surround you. To the degree that you can train your brain to be aware of the positives and therefore "achieve happiness," you will be able to change your behavior pattern. As a result, you can create significant cultural shifts in the larger world as well.

Shawn Achor, founder of the psychological consulting firm GoodThinkInc. and author of *The Happiness Advantage: The Seven Principles of Positive Psychology That Fuel Success and Performance at Work*, set out to study the top 10 percent of the happiest people in the world. Achor was surprised to find that these people were not happy all the time. Their moods fluctuated like those of most people. They just had much higher baselines than everyone else. That baseline is what we think of as our predisposition. By changing your mindset and habits, you can actually move your baseline up dramatically. You are not going to become someone who is happy all the time—no one is. But if you move your baseline up, your highs will be higher, and your lows will be higher too.

Take the old adage that if you work hard, you will be successful and happy. According to Achor, if you are happy and you work hard, you will have a higher level of success. Think about it. If you can actually increase your well-being and state of happiness today—in the midst of the challenges and the workload you face, in the midst of the struggling economy that we all face—then your success rate will rise dramatically. You will be able to work even harder, faster, and more intelligently than you already do.

In *The Happiness Advantage*, Achor describes a few simple steps you can follow for 21 days that will begin to retrain your brain. Those who have tested as low-level pessimists may suddenly begin to be significantly more positive.

Each day, when you wake up or first get to work, take 45 seconds to write down three things for which you are grateful. Before or after lunch or first thing in the morning, take two minutes to meditate. This need not be a formal meditation. Just sit quietly, breathe slowly and deeply, and try to clear your head of all the internal and external noise. Before you go to bed or leave the office, spend five minutes writing about one positive experience you had in the prior 24 hours. Finally, get some regular exercise. This does not have to be an extensive daily workout. Light exercise for just 15 to 20 minutes three times a week is sufficient. That is enough to release endorphins and train your brain to feel that you have been successful.

So what does this have to do with having successful Money Talks? According to Achor, who was a guest on my radio show, this kind of simple program can make Money Talks less stressful and more productive. When you bring a positive mental attitude to a discussion and deliver your point of view in a positive way, you will probably get a better outcome.

Maybe you are the point person to discuss estate-planning issues with your aging parents. If you have trained yourself to "see the glass half-empty" and expect your parents to reject your offers to help, then you will approach the situation without confidence and constructive energy. You might find that the conversation ends abruptly and unsatisfactorily. On the other hand, if you have put yourself in a positive state of mind, have carefully thought through and prepared for the discussion, and know how to make your points in a nonjudgmental way, the conversation is likely to go much better. And you will be able to think creatively and work through any challenges that might come up in the discussion.

Like other financial advisors, I have come across a few clients over the years who are unable to break a pattern of negative thinking or behavior. Tetris is a simple computer game in which players arrange shapes on a screen. For all its apparent simplicity, it is extraordinarily addictive. It is believed that the repetitive behavior involved in playing the game triggers something in the brain that encourages even more of the same behavior. Applying the phenomenon in the context of daily living, individuals who are unable to break a pattern of thinking or behaving are said to suffer from the "Tetris effect." An example would be a copyeditor who spends endless hours every day correcting manuscripts. After a period of time, the editor's brain becomes wired to look for mistakes in other parts of his life, including the actions of his spouse or his children. This could lead to problems in his relationships at home and in the office, as well as interfering with his ability to adapt to challenges and successfully navigate his life.

That's what happened to John Baranyi, a burly and outgoing 63-year-old CPA and successful real estate investor. John grew up very poor in a working-class neighborhood in the Northeast.

He lived with his older brother, Tony, and his parents, Albert and Adrienne, in a one-bedroom apartment on the third floor of a walk-up building. His father and mother, Hungarian immigrants, didn't speak English and struggled to make ends meet for John and Tony. Albert was a maintenance worker at the local school. Adrienne took in laundry for the neighbors.

John was the first in the family to go to college, winning a football scholarship to a state university. He married his college sweetheart, Carol, and they had two children, Lance and Lucas. Carol worked as an emergency room nurse at the local hospital. John rose to become partner at a major accounting firm. With his earnings and his savings, in the early 1970s he began investing in suburban real estate. A highly talented businessman and professional, he was able to participate with other partners in solid real estate investments with the potential for future cash flow. He invested the money he and Carol had saved from their earnings. His real estate business eventually became so successful that he quit his job as a managing partner at the accounting firm to manage his real estate investments full time.

Today, John and Carol have real estate investments that generate significant income. They also have a liquid portfolio resulting from the sale of properties over time. Their investment portfolio includes significant positions in equities, hedge funds, tax-exempt bonds, and cash and cash equivalents. Although John has more assets than he, his wife, and their two children will need in their lifetimes, he still does not feel financially safe or secure. Even though he is a highly intelligent man, he cannot remove himself from the mental state of poverty. This mindset pervaded his youth and his early experience with money. As a result, he filters all the information he receives to support his negative view of the world.

After speaking with John and Carol, I recommended that he stop listening to and reading the financial media. I promised him that I would provide him with information from reliable, non-fear-mongering sources and would help him understand the fundamental economic conditions and trends affecting the global markets. I promised to educate him on the types and levels of risk in the marketplace. I enlisted Carol's help to get him to start exercising and to better manage his daily stress.

Carol, who came from a solidly upper-middle-class Italian family from Chicago, never wanted for anything while she was growing up. She is a naturally upbeat and positive person. Each day, she instinctively embraces a sense of gratitude and is mindful of how blessed she and all her family are. At my urging, Carol is trying to encourage John to focus each day on the wonderful things in his life. So far, it seems that our efforts are working. John did not get emotionally overwhelmed by the most recent market volatility and appears to be developing a more optimistic overall long-term view.

Unfortunately, there are times when an individual's temperament is so difficult that no amount of help can prevent it from wreaking havoc on a family, financially and otherwise. This can sabotage money conversations and disrupt the financial and emotional health of the family. In my experience, people with problematic temperaments often "act out" upon the death of a family matriarch or patriarch. That was the case with the Ruben family.

Neil Ruben was a very successful architect, known for his designs of corporate headquarters in the suburbs of New York. His wife, Rose, died of breast cancer at 60 and left her assets in trusts and partnerships to Neil. The largest portion of those assets was in family partnerships in which the Rubens's three children and two nieces held varying interests. Neil and Rose's eldest daughter, Katherine, has always been a domineering person. When her mother died, Katherine felt that she should automatically assume the role of family matriarch and take charge of the lives of the rest of the family. Katherine suffered from clinical depression that had contributed to a drinking problem and two failed marriages. None of that kept her from trying to control the lives of her siblings and cousins.

Neil died of a massive coronary just prior to the real estate collapse of 2008. Katherine was the only member of the family who was surprised that Neil had not named her as executor of his estate, which was quite substantial, or as successor managing partner of the family partnerships. Instead, these roles were given to the middle son, Adam, and a trusted business associate. Although the market crash had severely reduced the value of the estate's holdings, Katherine fought as if she were battling for control of the crown jewels. In her mind, I suppose, she was, since she felt that the true crown jewel was being named the heir apparent.

Katherine hired an attorney and fought the estate plan. Only after she had cost the family thousands of dollars in legal fees was the case thrown out, leaving the financial state of the partnerships even worse off than before, and ensuring that she was estranged, perhaps permanently, from the rest of the family.

Different Generations Lead to Different Attitudes Toward Money

You typically do not speak to your 76-year-old mother, your 42-year-old sister, and your 15-year-old daughter in the same way. And that is not simply because of your different relationships with them. Age is a factor that we seldom focus on when we think about how we communicate with the members of our family about money and everything else.

We are living in unprecedented times. As a result of medical breakthroughs, people are living longer. That means that many of us are in families or workplaces in which multiple generations interact.

We have the "greatest generation," or those who were born before 1946, who lived through two world wars; the invention of cars, movies, and airplanes; and the Great Depression. Identified as "traditionalists," they believe in a strong work ethic, that life is uncertain, and that you have to be prepared for what the future may bring.

Then there are the baby boomers, born between 1946 and 1964, who grew up during the post-World War II economic boom. They internalized the upward-mobility message of "a house for every family and a car in every garage." Through the invention of TV, the end of the Vietnam War, the lunar landing, civil rights, and women's rights, they learned that they could make a difference and change the world through activism. However, that activism faded, and many baby boomers emerged over time as self-indulgent, materialistic, and obsessed with their careers.

Next are the generation Xers. Born between 1965 and 1980, they lived through Watergate, the Iran Contra scandals, AIDS, and skyrocketing divorce rates. Many of them were latchkey kids, as their mothers entered the workforce en masse. These experiences shaped their skepticism about every institution—from government to marriage—and their intense independence, adaptability, and resourcefulness. Gen Xers enjoy both work and life. They are focused on balancing the two, much more so than their parents.

Finally, we have generation Y or the millennials, born between 1981 and 2000. Their formative experiences include Columbine, 9/11, Hurricanes Katrina and Rita, the domination of information technology, and the globalization of the economy. These experiences have resulted in high rates of volunteerism and voting, as well as communication and connectivity. Because of their intimacy with technology, they think work and life are one and the same.

Think about how the age factor affects conversations among individuals from these four very different generations. Most obviously, the preferred means of communication differ dramatically from generation to generation. Members of the greatest generation prefer communicating face to face or through snail mail. The preferred means of communication for most baby boomers are face to face or via telephone. Gen Xers grew up using e-mail and embraced cellular telephones. And millennials prefer texting and communicating via Facebook posts. If you are a baby boomer, your younger siblings and children may be very uncomfortable with extended face-to-face conversations, while your parents may be unable to deal with electronic communications. Millennials, regardless of gender, are also adept at multitasking and are often uncomfortable when they have to give their undivided attention to one "input." You need to consider how these different preferences affect Money Talks and plan accordingly, perhaps sending meeting schedules to your parents via snail mail, to your siblings over the phone or via e-mail, and to your children via text or Facebook. You will also need to insist that all smartphones are turned off and stored away during the Money Talk.

The language you use can also impact the conversation either positively or negatively. Each generation has a different vocabulary associated with money based on life experiences and levels of education. It is best to use language that is age appropriate for the generation you are engaging with in the money conversation. When discussing technical topics, I recommend that you avoid using legal terms that can be intimidating and can contribute to generational divides.

Regardless of which generation you represent, your world was dramatically different from your parents' world, and the world into which your children and your grandchildren were born is profoundly different from the world in which you were raised. And, when it comes to having a money conversation, it is critical to understand that each generation has a different relationship with money. For instance, those born before 1945 experienced the worst economic depression in the history of this country and a war in which more than 400,000 Americans' lives were lost. The struggles related to those experiences made them cautious and frugal and led them to live below their means. Compare that with baby boomers, who were raised on the principles of Dr. Spock during a postwar economic boom. They are often spendthrifts, feeling that they deserve to have whatever they desire. Theirs is the generation that spawned the bumper sticker, "He Who Dies with the Most Toys Wins" and that became the darlings of Madison Avenue advertisers, who quickly learned ways to "encourage" them to spend.

Generational differences in values and experiences also affect philanthropic decisions. Because individuals from the greatest generation are living longer, they are working side by side with millennials in family foundations. Each group needs to understand the different motivations for charitable giving, according to Sharna Goldseker, vice president of the Andrea and Charles Bronfman Philanthropies, where she directs 21/64, a nonprofit consulting practice specializing in next-generation and multigenerational strategic philanthropy.

Traditionalists, says Goldseker, have values that were created at a time when loyalty, patriotism, and faith were rewarded. Baby boomers competed for and won leadership positions in family charitable organizations. They then began resisting gen Xers, who have been anxiously waiting their turn. Though gen Xers were only in their twenties or thirties, many of them entered management positions at young ages and never had to compete for leadership roles. Their ambition to lead family philanthropies, notes Goldseker, sometimes comes across as disrespect. Finally, the millennials, bolstered by the connectivity afforded them through technology and having an incredible tolerance for diversity, have strong ideas about giving. Remarkably, this youngest generation is often a voice of reason among all the generations at the family philanthropy table.

Eileen and Jon Gallo, a psychotherapist and estate attorney who jointly wrote *Silver Spoon Kids: How Successful Parents Raise Responsible Children*, suggest that each individual develops a unique three-dimensional relationship with money that includes money acquisition, money use, and money management. This three-dimensional relationship is developed as a result of the messages received as children and how the mind organizes the information. Because every generation develops at a different time in a different environment, it receives different messages and learns to organize those messages differently. If you were to compare the approaches to money acquisition, money use, and money management among generations, you would see very different relationships with money. By looking closely at those relationships with money, you may also be able to explain family financial patterns and behaviors, which I will explore later in this chapter.

Every financial advisor has a favorite story about generational differences in money attitudes. The client whose story always comes first to my mind is Claire O'Brian. Claire is an 86-year-old widow with an infectious smile and a trace of the brogue she brought with her from Ireland. Her late husband was a successful restaurant entrepreneur who left her with significant assets, enough to allow her to fully enjoy her life. But because of her experience growing up poor, first in Ireland and then here during the Great Depression, Claire lives on the budget of a church mouse. While she is capable of gifting some of her assets to her three children and seven grandchildren and could benefit taxwise from doing so, she was not ready to consider it when she and I began making her estate plan.

In order to get Claire to begin to think about giving away her money, I suggested ways to reduce the tax bill that would be due at her death and that would significantly reduce her assets. I pointed out that she would also be helping to ensure the future of the grandchildren she adores. Cash flow was not an issue. In fact, Claire refused to take all the income that her portfolio generated, preferring to keep a healthy cash balance—definitely a sign of money insecurity.

My money conversations with Claire were initially slow and methodical. She is an intelligent woman, but she didn't have a sophisticated money vocabulary. Much of my time with her was spent giving her assurances that she would have more than enough assets to sustain her for the rest of her life. Over the course of a couple of years, I was able to make her feel comfortable with an aggressive gifting program as a way of preventing Uncle Sam from "inheriting" the assets she and her husband had worked so hard to accrue over a long period of time.

During our conversations, it became clear that Claire found fault with what she perceived to be her children's frivolous use of money. Her two sons, Liam and Sean, and her daughter, Molly, are professionals. Each is married to a hardworking, equally career-minded partner. Claire sees them spending money for vacations and carrying large mortgages, rather than saving one of their two incomes and preparing for the economic doom that she is sure will inevitably arrive. Luckily, Claire's children and their families have been largely unaffected by the most recent economic downturn. However, they are struggling with the cash flow constraints associated with maintaining their homes and their lifestyles while covering the education costs of their own children.

At Claire's request, and as a proviso of her moving forward with the gifting plan, I met with her children about their particular financial concerns. We eventually discussed the uncomfortable subject of Claire's opinion of their lifestyles and spending habits, and the importance of budgeting and spending more wisely. We spoke about redefining their needs versus their wants, but we also spent a lot of time talking about generational attitudes toward money.

My hope was to help them understand why Claire was often so critical of their approach to money. The goal was to give them a greater understanding of her generation's unique struggles, increase their sensitivity to her personal history and experience, and, as a result, improve their Money Talks. We also discussed why it was important to demonstrate discipline with money, not only as a way of improving their own financial picture, but as a way of transmitting healthy money values to their children. I encouraged them to have ongoing conversations with their own children using language they could relate to, and promoted the notion of allowances as a way to help educate and create value around money using the Rockefeller model, which consists of three components: saving, spending, and sharing.

Over the months, Claire, her children, and her grandchildren have come to realize that they approach money from different perspectives. We have had a number of healthy Money Talks. I think they have laid the foundation for finally starting to address the issues of generational wealth transfer in a productive, nonconfrontational manner. I am optimistic about the direction they are taking.

Everyone's Family History Affects Money Behavior

Each individual brings her unique family history, rooted in generations of experience, to every conversation. Typically, as we communicate with others throughout the day, we operate in the present moment and think only about the issue, topic, or task at hand. But it probably is not too difficult for you to recall a recent conversation in which you found yourself overreacting, responding to the other person with more emotion than was appropriate to the situation. While there may certainly be countless reasons for such a reaction, family history is often the cause.

Many people have unresolved emotional or psychological issues from their past that bubble up to the surface when they find themselves in difficult conversations. People who instinctively handle these stressful conversations with grace and ease probably had healthy family role models who communicated effectively without overreacting. Those of us who have not been raised with the tools to handle such conversations need to acquire them through some combination of trial and error, guidance from advisors with experience and skill in communicating, and working through the family issues that are typically at the root of overreactions.

Whatever messages we get as children—whether they are about money or about other topics—are repeated through the generations. The three dimensions that Eileen and Jon Gallo wrote about—money acquisition, money use, and money management—form patterns that, while not identical, have recurring themes and similarities. These intergenerational patterns are nurtured in children at very young ages and are woven into the fabric of the family. Suppose your grandfather was a gambler and your grandmother was extremely conservative and worked hard to preserve the family finances. Your mother may have adopted messages of frugality from her mother, who never knew whether there was going to be enough money to take care of the family. Now you find yourself saving more than spending and constantly searching for the best bargain. Your grandmother's money values have been passed down to you, even though you are of a different generation and your economic circumstances may be different.

Early childhood messages certainly affected how Phyllis Stanton lived her adult life. A fit, trim, well-respected 48-year-old dermatologist, she is a single mom to 18-year-old Julia. Phyllis grew up in a dysfunctional home. The oldest of five children, she took charge of the family at the age of 13 when her mother, Anne, showed signs of alcoholism. A smart, savvy woman who had excelled in college, Anne was bored and restless as a stay-at-home mom. She had been unable to exercise much control in her family life, including the family finances. As her sense of worthlessness increased, so did her drinking. And as her drinking increased, Anne began to abdicate most of the childcare and household responsibilities, the only areas over which she still had some influence, to Phyllis.

Arthur, Phyllis's father, was an ambitious and tremendously successful global marketing executive for a Fortune 500 company.

He kept a tight rein on the family finances. Each month he deposited a paltry amount into an account that Anne used to run the household and care for the children. It was never enough to meet the family's needs adequately. Married to his job, he traveled on business several weeks out of every month. As he became aware of Anne's problems, Arthur looked to his teenage daughter Phyllis to keep the household running while he was away. But the family conflict made this increasingly difficult. When Arthur was home, the relationship between him and Anne was always tense, with little communication between them. Arthur didn't involve himself much with the family, and Anne was angry and resentful at her husband's lack of interest and his control of the family finances. Explosive arguments were the norm in the Stanton household. By the time Phyllis graduated from college, her parents had divorced.

Phyllis got married in her late twenties after graduating from medical school and joining a lucrative private dermatology practice in the Philadelphia area. Her husband, Edward, was a pharmaceutical sales rep who covered a large geographic region and frequently traveled for sales calls. While Edward earned a good living, Phyllis outearned him significantly. Because of her family history, she was driven to control her own destiny and never have to rely on a man for her financial needs. These income disparities and Phyllis's drive for financial independence were issues that the two of them never openly discussed. With both of them climbing the career ladder, they had little time to establish a healthy and ongoing dialogue about issues that mattered.

Once their daughter, Julia, was born, conversations became all about logistics. Like Phyllis's father, Edward took little interest in family dynamics, yet he wanted to exert control over the family money. Phyllis became angry and resentful, as her mother had done. The family history and patterns around money that she had wanted to escape instead emerged in full force. Arguments became the norm in their household as well. After 12 years, the fabric of the marriage had torn, and Phyllis and Edward decided to divorce. Phyllis went into therapy and began to understand how the dynamics in her home when she was growing up had been repeated in the home she created with Edward. While it was too late to save her marriage, Phyllis began to learn the necessary skills to have healthy and productive conversations about money issues without the bubbling anger that had always interfered in the past.

While Phyllis's newfound communication skills and a skilled mediator made the divorce process less painful, a number of financial issues needed to be resolved. Phyllis decided to buy out Edward's share of the house. Julia would continue to live with her. Edward would still need to pay some child support, even though Phyllis was earning more than he was. Solving the college funding issue was more complicated. Though Julia was only 10 when they divorced, Edward and Phyllis agreed to contribute equal amounts to a Section 529 plan for Julia's benefit. The divorce decree required equal participation from both for the obligation of a four-year education. Phyllis's father had created a trust for Julia's benefit, but he was unwilling to release a portion of the funds until she turned 25, a painful legacy of his desire to maintain control. Phyllis never really kept track of the monies in the Section 529 that her ex-husband had created, and just assumed that Edward was contributing. It later turned out that he was not putting away an equal amount, but rather was contributing about one-quarter of what Phyllis had contributed.

When Julia was planning to attend college in a couple of years, it was time for Phyllis to take a close look at the college fund. She did not like what she saw. The fund had taken a hit during the financial crisis and had not fully recovered. While there was enough to pay for the first two years of college, Phyllis became concerned that there would not be enough money to send Julia to the school of her choice for all four years. She and Edward together hired a financial advisor and asked him to mediate a conversation between them. Phyllis knew that her historical anger and resentment toward her father and now her ex-husband for their lack of involvement in their families and their insistence on controlling the family finances could derail her ability to have an effective Money Talk.

With the advisor's help, Edward was able to assess his personal financial situation more clearly and commit to an automatic investment program that would transfer money directly to Julia's college fund. While the amount still was not equal to what Phyllis was contributing, it was significantly more than he had previously paid. The advisor also developed a more effective approach to the monies in the fund and made sure that all three spoke about the issue on a quarterly basis. Phyllis was able to defuse some of her anger, understand that Edward was doing the best he could, and accept that she might need to be the major contributor to helping her daughter possibly pay for graduate school.

There Are Cultural Differences in How People Approach Money

Culture refers to the way people think, feel, and act. Geert Hofstede, a well-known researcher of cross-cultural groups and organizations, and author of several books, including *Cultures and Organizations: Software of the Mind*, has defined culture as "the collective programming of the mind distinguishing the members of one group or category of people from another." Category, in Hofstede's definition, can refer to nations, regions within or across nations, ethnicities, religions, occupations, organizations, genders, and even members of a nuclear family.

How did we acquire collective cultural programming? Not surprisingly, the clinical/organizational psychologist Dr. Hendrie Weisinger believes that human culture is the result of hundreds of thousands of years of evolution. Though competition among groups of huntergatherers was a powerful evolutionary pressure that resulted in increased social and intellectual skills, we didn't lose those behaviors that identified us as social mammals. Fights for dominance, competition for partners, and wishes to belong and to know who does not belong are all basic drives that are still alive in us.

Culture revolves around issues of group membership, authority, gender roles, morality, anxiety, emotions, and drives. Not unlike family history, culture affects every aspect of our lives. We each acquire most of our programming during early childhood, when we have an incredible capacity to absorb information and follow examples from our social environment. This includes not just our parents and siblings, but also other elders and our playmates. All human groups, from the nuclear family to society, develop cultures as they go; this is what enables a group to function smoothly.

While each individual is unique in personality, history, and interest, everyone shares the common human nature of being hugely social. We are, after all, group animals. We use language and empathy, and we practice collaboration and intergroup competition, but the unwritten rules of how we do these things differ from one human group to another. Hofstede believes that culture consists of the unwritten rules about how to be a good member of the group.

Skills in cooperation across cultures are vital for our common survival—both in large multinational corporations and in small nuclear and extended families. Just take a look at America's changing demographic trends. More than half of the growth in the total U.S. population between 2000 and 2010 resulted from the increase in the Hispanic population, according to the 2010 U.S. Census. The Hispanic population grew by 43 percent in the last decade, surpassing 50 million and accounting for about one in six Americans. The Asian population is also growing at a surprisingly fast rate, moving from about 4 percent of the U.S. population in 2000 to about 6 percent in 2010. African Americans represent about 14 percent of the total population. The non-Hispanic white population is still the majority, although its proportion of the total U.S. population fell to 64 percent from 69 percent between 2000 and 2010. A 2008 Census Bureau projection estimates that ethnic and racial minorities will become the majority in the United States by 2042. Intercultural cooperation skills are vital when you consider how much we have moved from being a homogeneous community to being a heterogeneous community. Today we are not just working with but also marrying people from different ethnic, religious, geographic, or economic backgrounds more frequently.

While it is essential that we accept and understand cultural differences based on ethnic background, it is also necessary to realize that there are important cultural differences between recent immigrants and long-term citizens, regardless of their ethnic, religious, or geographic background.

Historically, first-generation immigrants are often focused on providing a better life for their children—at all costs. In some instances, they are uneducated and struggle with the new language. Others are highly educated and skilled professionals who left their native countries in search of political and economic freedom. If they arrive in this country poor and without education or transferrable skills, or if they are unable to regain the economic or professional status of their former lives, they may work at several low-paying jobs or jobs below their previous station. They may earn just enough to allow them to live, put their kids through school, and retire. They often lack trust in institutions and keep large holdings of cash, because it is a tangible asset. Their interest in financial vehicles is limited by their desire and their need to just put their money in a bank.

The second generation, the children, is more assimilated into American culture. These kids attend U.S. schools and see first-hand through their peers what money can buy. They understand that the path to financial success is often through education. Trust in financial markets and institutions increases with knowledge. This generation raises a third generation that is usually fully assimilated.

Fernando Gonzales is a classic second-generation American. He was born in San Antonio, Texas, the youngest of the three children of Maria and Carlos, a hardworking and impoverished couple who emigrated from Guadalajara, Mexico. Fernando's childhood home was made of flimsy cardboard-quality material. He lived in an ethnically and socioeconomically mixed neighborhood in which poor African Americans and Hispanics lived in close proximity to middle-class and wealthy whites.

As a boy, Fernando always had jobs, from working as a gas station attendant to managing a warehouse after he graduated from high school. His parents pushed him and his siblings to set lofty goals for themselves and to get the necessary education to escape the poverty from which they had been unable to break free.

Fernando's mother had gone to work as a housekeeper in Canada when she was young and had sent money home to support her family. She was the most prominent influence in Fernando's life and always stressed that education was the ticket out of poverty. Fernando heard the message loud and clear.

After serving in the military during the Vietnam War, Fernando returned and enrolled in college. He received a scholarship from a local bank where he had worked part time. This, along with federal loans, enabled him to pay for his undergraduate degree at a prestigious southern university. Upon graduation, Fernando went back to work for the bank that had provided him the opportunity. The bank subsequently paid for him to attend graduate school, and ultimately he received his MBA.

Today, Fernando is a very successful private banker with a major U.S. banking institution. His wife, Monica, who came from a background similar to Fernando's, gave up a marketing position at the bank to stay home to raise their two daughters. Fernando and Monica are very involved in a local organization that provides college scholarships to underprivileged Hispanic kids.

Given their poor upbringing, it is no surprise that Fernando and Monica are extremely careful about spending. They are big savers and consistently live beneath their means. Because of the exemplary lifestyle they lead and the volunteer work they do, the two of them serve as good role models for their children. The message Fernando received from his mother, that education is key, was passed on to his children. Both of his kids went to college and are succeeding on their own.

Fernando had very few Money Talks as a child. Other than an annual Christmas gift of school clothes, he worked to pay for everything extra he wanted. Today he has a different approach with his children. He believes that Money Talks are necessary, and he started them when he thought the girls were old enough not to be spoiled by the information. Fernando's younger daughter is still not entirely comfortable with the Money Talks, since she associates them with the death of her parents. Still, while she and her sister may not know the specifics of each investment or account, they know where all the documents and accounts are located and the approximate valuations. The girls have also met with the family attorney, whom the family trusts to step in should anything happen to Fernando or Monica.

Fernando and Monica are classic examples of the cultural immigrant experience in America's melting pot. Fernando's family history and the emphasis on education also illustrate the cultural and generational patterns that he acquired from his mother and that he passed down to his kids.

The impact of the immigrant experience on money attitudes is so pronounced that it can divide couples who otherwise would appear to have a shared culture. That was the case with Ramona and Frank Mills. Both work at a prestigious Illinois university: Frank as a professor of history, and Ramona as an administrator in the student affairs department.

Ramona was born in Jamaica and came to the United States with the rest of her family when she was 15. Her father was a government official in Jamaica, and her mother was a schoolteacher. Looking to give their five children a better life, they moved to Chicago, where they had extended family. Ramona's father worked in construction and her mother cleaned houses in order to help put all five of their children through college. Their children were raised to avoid debt, other than student loans, and to pay cash for everything. Ramona's parents bought their very modest home for cash and never had credit cards.

Frank's family was also from Jamaica originally. But it was his great-grandparents who were the immigrants. Immigrant ideals and tendencies had been diluted by the time Frank was born. His father was a well-known newspaper columnist and his mother the headmistress of a private school. The family was upper middle class, lived in a famously integrated suburb of Chicago, and had a fully developed financial life. Frank grew up to be as comfortable with borrowing and debt as any other third- or fourth-generation American.

After Frank and Ramona were married, their cultural differences were first expressed in their purchase of a home. Frank thought nothing of taking out as large a mortgage as possible in order to buy as expensive a home as they could afford. Ramona, on the other hand, was aghast at the idea of assuming so much debt and instead wanted to wait to buy a home until they had sufficient money saved, and then to buy something that Frank thought was beneath their means. She was already anxious about how much Frank put on his credit card, and the thought of a 30-year mortgage terrified her. Eventually, thanks to some heart-to-heart Money Talks, they were able to compromise. Frank convinced her of the wisdom of taking out a 30-year mortgage, but agreed that they would put 30 percent down and would avoid risky variable-rate loans. And he agreed to use his credit card only in emergencies.

Another cultural difference that is often ignored is geography.

Joe Mathews is a handsome, outgoing midwesterner. As a result of his career as financial manager for a major technology company, he has lived in three different parts of the country. An intelligent and engaging person, Joe valued his ability to observe and adapt to the regional cultural mores, which differed with regard to money.

Joe was raised in a small, rural Michigan town in the 1960s. His father sold farm equipment. Deals were struck with a handshake. If a contract was necessary to seal the deal, trust waned. If fast talk entered the conversation, then the lack of trust became uncomfortably high. Joe's mom was a substitute teacher at the local high school and a volunteer at the local church, where she taught Sunday school.

Joe's parents, like most of the people in his town, were unassuming and down-to-earth. Although they could afford to own a fancy car or take good vacations, they chose not to live an affluent lifestyle. The culture of nonurban areas in the Midwest was not to wear your worth on your shirtsleeves and not to stand out. It was important to conform, to "fit in" at all costs and remain part of the community.

As a result, no one really knew how much money anyone had, and the M Word was off limits for discussion. Joe never had a Money Talk with his parents until he started to think about college. After a discussion of all the various costs associated with different schools, his parents told him that there would be tuition money for four years, as long as he worked during the summers to earn the money for his living expenses. Joe was pleasantly surprised. He had been told from the time he was 10 that if he wanted something, he would have to go out and earn the money to pay for it. Joe did not have another Money Talk with his parents until his father was about to retire and approached Joe for some financial advice.

Joe thinks the understatement of wealth by people in his small town was in part tied to the act of tithing, which was expected of church members. If people came to church in a Mercedes or wore expensive clothing, they would be expected to give more money when the basket was passed. There was an assumption that their earnings or assets had increased and that if they didn't increase their contributions, they were not giving their fair share to the church. Joe's mom was particularly devoted to tithing, and each year she and her husband would donate 10 percent of their earnings to the church. It was the tradition of tithing in his family that became the foundation for Joe's charitable activities today.

Joe then moved to southern California, where he lived among young families, relocated retirees, and well-to-do families who had lived there for at least a generation. He observed that these people had a very different relationship with money from the one he had seen at home. People spent freely and were not tied to the cultural norms he had experienced in the rural Midwest. They were more relaxed and balanced in their lives. They just seemed more open and upbeat.

Not long after arriving, Joe met and married Sally, a native Californian whose father was a wealthy owner of a number of restaurant franchises. She had a sunny disposition and enjoyed life to the fullest. They bought a house with her dad's help, and within a few years, Sally gave birth to her first child, a beautiful baby girl who looked just like Joe and had her warm disposition and smile.

Other regional differences struck Joe. He was quite surprised by the openness with which Sally discussed money with him and the willingness of her family to discuss the topic. Sally's dad, now 85, had regular family meetings with her and her two brothers, who were in the family real estate business. He would discuss the current state of his estate plan, his retirement plans, and the decisions he had made that would involve each of them. He told them where the original documents were located and provided a complete list of all his advisors. He also told them of the roles each would play, from successor executors to trustees to shareholders in a family limited liability corporation (LLC). He explained the details of the gifting program he had designed around the LLC. The LLC owned real estate and business interests from which his kids and future grandkids would benefit.

Sally's dad also explained that he had created a portfolio of liquid assets in a trust. He told his children that he would be gifting each of them monies so that they could learn how to manage money and work with advisors. Sally's dad was quite comfortable taking a passive role and letting his advisors oversee a professionally managed portfolio. Having lived on the West Coast for his entire life, he admitted that he was quite far removed from the financial center in New York City and knew nothing about trading his own securities. He preferred to focus on the long-term planning issues with his advisory team, which consisted of his lawyer, his accountant, and his financial advisor.

Joe and Sally spent several years in California, where Joe learned to appreciate the open communication that Sally's family enjoyed. The couple then moved to Texas when Joe's company transferred him there. Once again, Joe experienced a remarkably different culture from that of his hometown.

The most obvious cross-cultural difference that Joe noticed was in speech speed and conversational style. Deborah Tannen, in her book *I Say This Because I Love You*, notes that people in different regions speak at different rates of speed. Individuals from slower-speaking regions are often stereotyped as unintelligent, and those from fast-talking regions are stereotyped as aggressive. An example of this stereotyping in the United States is how people perceive New Yorkers as brash and southerners as polite.

Joe found that Texans were less than trusting of fast-talking salespeople and without question did not fit the image of the unintelligent slow talker. He realized very quickly that he had to be careful and slow down his speech. He also learned that Texans liked to talk openly about deal-making opportunities and viewed themselves as independent and self-reliant. Joe made friends with some Texas entrepreneurs who were engaged in investing in oil and gas, agriculture, and real estate. Like the Californians, they openly discussed these financial matters, albeit at a slower pace.

Cultural issues are perhaps the most complex of the hidden obstacles to a successful Money Talk. They rarely translate as simply as male versus female, or baby boomer versus millennial. They are often overlooked, frequently multilayered with other issues, and always unique.

Consider the case of Li Zhang. She moved from China to the United States when she was a child. She says that she has an undeniably Chinese attitude toward money, but if you read below the surface, you can see it is equally an immigrant attitude. Li says that in China, frugality is a virtue. As a result, Chinese people are always looking for a bargain, and haggling is a way of life. She says that Chinese people regularly save 50 to 60 percent of their income, and that to them cash is king.

One trait Li identifies as Chinese does indeed seem to be distinct from the typical money culture. Chinese people, she says, have no problem sharing their salaries. It is not rude or a bad thing in the Chinese culture to talk about money.

That is an approach I think every other culture would do well to consider.

I know this chapter has covered a great deal of territory, much of which is rarely discussed. If there is one underlying message that I want you to take away from this wide-ranging discussion, it is the importance of awareness. Armed with knowledge about the elements that make money such a difficult topic to discuss, you will at the very least be emotionally and psychologically prepared for your next Money Talk. In the following chapter, we will address the physical logistics of the Money Talk: setting the stage for the meeting and where, when, and how to have it.

Things to Think About

- Who in your family needs to have control? Why do you think that is?
- Whom in your family do you trust? Why?
- How has the presence or absence of trust affected your family's financial planning and communications?
- Can you characterize the roles each of your immediate family members play in the family? Is there a dominant personality? Is there a demanding family member? Is there an emotionally absent family member? Is there one sibling who is the achiever and one who is the ne'er-do-well?
- How have gender differences affected conversations about money with your colleagues or friends?
- What gender differences have you observed when it comes to money?
- Can you think of times when you or members of your family have reacted reflectively about money and times when you have reacted reflexively?
- Do you make decisions slowly and deliberately or fast and furiously? Does that apply across the board, or only to one aspect of your life?
- Do you have a financial plan and an investment strategy in place? If you do, has it worked for you in times of intense volatility?
- Are you aware of the role that instincts play in your daily behavior and conversations?
- When you have had difficult conversations in the past, have you done anything to create a pleasing environment or worked at using the right words?
- How does your personal temperament affect your communication and actions?

(continued)

- Are you a pessimist or an optimist? Is that true across the board, or is it true of just one aspect of your life: work, personal life, or money, for example?
- What do you do, if anything, to stay optimistic or become more so? Are there any actions you take to create a positive attitude?
- How have generational differences affected your communication at work or socially?
- What are the family history and cultural differences that are at play when you are dealing with your family members?
- How would you describe your family's culture? Do you think this primarily comes from ethnic or national background, sociological factors, geography, or some other circumstances?

9

Preparation Pays

What Is the Agenda for Your Money Talk?

He who fails to plan, plans to fail.
—Winston Churchill

The drum roll, please. The suspense I feel when I am reaching the climactic conclusion of a long-anticipated event is similar to how I feel about this chapter. Everything I have covered so far has been paving the way to get you to this point—that is, to have the Money Talk, the face-to-face conversation about finances with your family. But if you now just dial or text your siblings or your parents and launch into a heart-to-heart discussion, you will be gravely disappointed with the outcome. Just as we drilled down to understand why the conversation is so difficult, to determine the transition points in your life that require it, and to explore the psychological and emotional factors percolating under the surface that interfere with it, we need to approach the critical step of actually engaging in the conversation with the same level of due diligence.

Think of this process as the staging of a play. It's one that, given all the subtext we noted in Chapter 3, can resemble a Shakespearean drama. Producing a staged event of any kind, particularly one that can be emotionally charged, often takes months of preparation and planning. While many of you may think it is overkill to make such an analogy, I cannot emphasize enough the importance of the necessary planning and preparation to encourage and fuel an open discussion and ultimately achieve the result you are seeking. That is because today it is more difficult than ever before to craft a face-to-face conversation.

The advent of connective technology such as e-mail, texting, tweeting, and Facebook has led our conversation skills to atrophy. We are substituting technology-driven conversations for human connections. "We are together, but each of us is in our own bubble, furiously connected to keyboards and tiny touch screens," wrote Sherry Turkle, a psychologist, MIT professor, and author of *Alone Together: Why We Expect More from Technology and Less from Each Other*. In an April 2012 *New York Times* article, "The Flight from Conversation," she wrote, "Human relationships are rich; they're messy and demanding. We have learned the habit of cleaning them up with technology." But conversation is more than connection. It is an art that requires patience and skill . . . and preparation.

Whether or not you need to consider the impact of technology use on the conversational abilities of those who will participate in the Money Talk, the process remains the same. It just becomes even more important if any or all of the participants are more comfortable typing to others rather than talking to each other.

The first stage in your planning should focus on everything that happens before you sit in the room with your family member or members and have the crucial conversation. This part of the process encompasses all the what, who, where, when, and how questions. Answering some of those may initially appear simple, but in reality, it can be quite difficult.

No doubt there was a catalyst that made you realize that you need to have this all-important discussion. Did you just have a baby? Has your oldest child moved back home after college? Is your spouse looking to retire in the next year? Is your surviving parent having health issues, and is he in need of an update to both his estate plan and his living situation? All these questions get back to identifying the transition point you are experiencing in your life. Sound familiar? This was the subject of Chapter 2. Except now, before you begin to fully explore the issues and topics that arise during the transition point, you need to collect and crystallize your thoughts about why you need to have the Money Talk and what you want to accomplish. You need to drill down and identify your goals for the conversations. What are you trying to achieve? It will be much easier to speak to your family members about money if you are clear about your reasons for doing so.

Once you have pinpointed the reasons, articulated your objectives for initiating the conversation, and identified the transition point that served as the catalyst, you can begin to think more deeply about all the issues and topics that surround the event. I recommend that you document your thoughts, your goals, and the issues and topics on paper or in a text file. The act of documenting them can help you to define and articulate them more clearly. And the document can also serve as a tool to support your verbal communications with family members and advisors.

For example, if you are just starting a family, you may be concerned with how you can best provide financial security for your children. If your first child was recently born, you have probably already thought about the basic daily needs of the new addition to the family. Will a parent stay at home? Will the kids go to childcare? Will you hire a nanny? But now there are new topics that have arisen as a result of the baby's birth that are longer-term in nature. Do you need life insurance to secure her future along with that of your spouse or partner? Do you plan to pay or borrow for her college education, or will there be some help from family members? How do you plan to save? And what about your will? If this is your first child, who will be the guardian or trustee? How does this new arrival affect the updating or revision of your existing estate plan, if you have one already?

Or maybe there has been a death in the family and a problematic sibling is acting more irrationally than usual at a time when there are a myriad of issues that need to be tackled methodically. You can imagine all the topics and details that need to be discussed: the details of the will, the communications and meetings with the attorney and the accountant, the steps associated with proper probating and settling of the estate, the distribution of estate and trust assets, the filing of the estate return, and the payment of the required taxes. You may have questions surrounding the impact that the inheritance will have on your life. What if you have a complaint about how the family monies are being distributed? How can you lodge such a complaint? Often most sensitive of all, how will you and your siblings divide up personal assets such as the baby grand piano and grandma's art collection?

Whatever the situation you are facing, documenting all the questions and concerns you have will help guide you through the process and ensure that you tackle each issue along the way. Once you have fully explored the objectives and issues surrounding your specific life event, you need to be thinking about the management of the Money Talk: who should be party to the conversation; where should it take place; when is the best time of the year, month, and day to have the talk; and what is the best way to conduct it so that the conversation meets your objectives while encouraging family harmony and preserving the family finances? Setting up and facilitating a Money Talk is by no means an easy task. But do not let the difficulty of the mission become a rationalization for procrastinating or an excuse for not holding the Money Talk at all. You already know it is a vital task, and having reached this point, you have already learned how to recognize the most daunting hurdles. You have come too far to give up now.

Noah and Barbara Stein did not let the obstacles deter them. The transition point that precipitated their desire to have a Money Talk with their four adult children was Barbara's being diagnosed with a rare form of cancer. There was tremendous uncertainty surrounding her illness. The doctors were unsure about how aggressive the cancer would be and whether an experimental treatment would work. Even though Noah and Barbara, both in their mid-seventies, had done a significant amount of advance estate planning, they had yet to share their thinking and their plans with their children. They knew they needed to have a Money Talk that communicated their plan for the transfer of their estate to their kids and grandchildren. They also recognized they would need to have repeated family meetings to discuss other topics related to the transfer of wealth to their heirs. These topics would include such issues as new responsibilities, family values, mission and governance, possible marital issues, and ongoing education.

Ironically, considering the family's emphasis on financial literacy and education, Noah and Barbara had never shared much about their financial plans with the kids. Noah, a stocky man with a full head of silver hair and wire-rim glasses, had begun his working life as an internist, but after returning to school to receive his MBA from a prestigious institution, through a series of jobs, he evolved into a prominent money manager whose specialty was finding biotech jewels to invest in long and short. The couple eventually settled in San Francisco, where Noah founded his own firm. As a result of his success in investing in both private and public companies, they were able to sock away quite a bit of money that they hoped to pass on to their kids one day. Barbara, a slim, athletic woman with shoulder-length brunette hair and green eyes, was a well-known anthropology professor at a local university. None of their children, three girls and one boy, had settled near their parents in the San Francisco area. The oldest, Daniel, had a PhD in biochemistry and worked as a biotechnology consultant. He was married and lived with his wife, a university professor, and two kids in southern California. Sandra, an international public policy specialist, lived in Geneva, Switzerland, with her author husband and their three kids. Janis was a nonpracticing attorney living in Ohio with her husband, a highly paid surgeon, and their three kids. And finally there was Denise, a yoga instructor, who was married to a carpenter and lived outside of Atlanta with her husband and their two kids.

Beginning in the kids' childhood and continuing to the present, Noah and Barbara made a point of hosting an annual intergenerational trip over the Christmas holidays to bring the family together and help maintain relationships at each generation level, particularly as the family members grew farther apart geographically. Because of their incredibly busy professional and personal lives, all the family members planned their schedules around this trip. On the surface, the siblings got along well enough. The annual trips had mostly been harmonious and fun affairs. But there were always longstanding tensions among the siblings bubbling under the surface.

There was the typical sibling rivalry between Sandra and Janis, who were only 20 months apart. While each of the older siblings had a soft spot in his or her heart for the youngest, Denise, there was some resentment because Noah and Barbara continuously provided financial support to Denise's family. The parents also contributed to maintaining the lifestyle of Sandra and her family, as her husband didn't earn much as an author. Daniel and Janis were the only two children who didn't rely on monies from their parents. As a result of all these arrangements, Barbara and Noah worried that this unequal treatment could become an issue, especially since everyone was already on edge as a result of Barbara's recent diagnosis. A couple whom they were both very close to had seen their family split apart when the differences in how children were treated financially were not disclosed and discussed.

The Steins began their planning by focusing on their motives— what they wanted for themselves, for their children, and for the family relationships. Their goals were to reduce their overall taxes, provide for a smooth transfer of assets during their lives and at their deaths, and try to perpetuate the kind of community and social involvement they had pursued throughout their own lives. They wanted to help their children and grandchildren as much as possible, but without unintentionally creating disincentives for them to work hard at their chosen pursuits. And they wanted to mitigate any turmoil between the siblings resulting from different treatment of them in the past, present, or future. Like all parents, they wanted to leave behind a family that was secure and intact, financially and emotionally.

The couple decided that the annual trip would be the best time to have the Money Talk. In an effort to think beyond the obvious and try to anticipate what problems might arise during the conversation, Noah wanted a location that would be favorably viewed by everyone, including the couple's financial advisor. The couple's primary advisor, Sharon, was an accountant, MBA, and Certified Financial Planner with short, wispy light brown hair, large tortoiseshell glasses, and a fondness for St. John suits. Noah and Barbara had worked with Sharon for nearly a decade, and she knew all the ins and outs of their estate plan as well as their investment portfolios. Sharon had also been through training on how to conduct family meetings and had experience doing just that with other clients who were addressing a broad range of transition points and topics. The Steins thought that Sharon's training and experience, and even just her presence as an impartial outsider, could help keep long-simmering annoyances from boiling over into outright conflict.

For this particular trip, the couple planned a family stay at an all-inclusive resort in Cabo San Lucas, Mexico. The 10 grandchildren ranged from 7 to 17 years old, and the resort had something for all of them. Noah and Barbara hoped that whatever tensions arose among the kids might be mitigated by everyone's being in a vacation state of mind and on neutral territory. Noah was afraid that if they had the talk at the family home, the location could trigger childhood issues and spark problems. They knew that past issues would not vanish, but they hoped that having everyone together in a relaxed, neutral setting would foster a sense of family unity and perhaps let everyone leave some of his or her psychological and emotional baggage behind.

Barbara and Noah regretted that they had waited until Barbara's cancer diagnosis to divulge their estate plan. They had always been waiting for a perfect time for the Money Talk, but then realized that there is never an ideal time to initiate a difficult-to-have conversation. Now it was absolutely imperative that they tackle the challenge. Going forward, they decided that the best strategy would be to schedule time to talk about estate-planning updates with the kids each year during the annual trip. Barbara and Noah decided to defer the decision to include additional outside counsel in future annual updates until they could see the outcome with the first one.

The couple usually e-mailed their kids in August to inform them where the annual vacation was to be held and when, so that all of them could mark their calendars. For this particular trip, they told their adult children that at least one day during the trip would include a family meeting and the Money Talk. They explained that for the initial meeting, it would be just the parents, the four adult children, and Sharon, who would act as moderator. Sharon warned Barbara and Noah that the process would probably take multiple conversations and meetings, but she explained that a plan would be formulated to address whatever issues were left outstanding after the first meeting. A follow-up Skype call could be made if necessary.

In their e-mail, Noah and Barbara asked each child to make sure that he or she came prepared with any questions about the estate transfer. They had already spoken to each child individually on the telephone about the purpose and content of the meeting, and as a result, they had a sense of what were the children's individual concerns. In preparation, they encouraged their kids to think through the financial, emotional, and psychological issues they faced. What were their financial needs, fears, and concerns, both for their family and individually? Because the entire family gathered only once a year, the couple also urged the kids to meet with their own advisors before the trip to discuss their concerns, their individual estate plans and any tax implications of an inheritance, and to draft a set of questions that could be asked.

Noah and Barbara took their own advice and met with Sharon a number of times prior to the Money Talk. They wanted to discuss what they hoped to accomplish, what they thought would be the ideal outcome, and what topics they would cover. In a coordinated team approach, orchestrated by Sharon with the family attorney and accountant, the Steins had created several trusts, including two generation-skipping trusts that had been funded using a portion of each of their estate exemptions and that contained life insurance as well as growth and income-producing securities. The intent was to provide funds for multiple generations, beginning with their adult children, to be used for housing, to supplement living expenses, to pay for the education of offspring, and to cover other expenses based on certain specifications established in the trusts. A makeup provision was included in the will to account for the noticeable disparity in the Steins's outlay of funds for the four children based on the needs of each. Several years ago, before Barbara's cancer had been diagnosed, they had placed their home in a qualified personal residence trust.[1] A second home had been placed in a separate trust. A family limited liability corporation had been created to hold various business interests and investment assets. Decisions concerning the management of the assets were carefully defined in the LLC document. Finally, Noah and Barbara had established and funded a family foundation. They were eager to have their children participate as board members and help with the management of the foundation and the decisions on distributing the funds annually to various charities that they and the grandchildren wished to support.

The Steins had always been philanthropic, donating to organizations that provided healthcare and education for the underserved. The value of charity had been ingrained in their kids, who had witnessed their parents' generosity over many years. As a result, the kids often participated in charitable causes on their own that they felt passionate about. Each had donated time or money to causes that were important to him or her. A family friend had established a foundation several years earlier, and had involved his kids in its ongoing management. He told the Steins the benefits that resulted. The process of working together to manage a family foundation had helped bring his three kids closer together, dissipated some of the sibling rivalry, and made each of them feel that he or she was an integral part of the process. They all seemed to benefit personally from being involved in the family's philanthropy.

In his book *Give to Live*, Dr. Douglas Lawson addresses the extraordinary physical, emotional, and psychological benefits that can come from giving and volunteering. He wrote of a 10-year study of 2,700 men in Michigan that found that those who did regular volunteer work had death rates 2½ times lower than those who did not. In a special government study of senior citizen activity as part of a 75-city research program, volunteers and the doctors who examined them reported that in 98 percent of the sites, the volunteers experienced measurable improvements in their physical and mental health.

Noah had had a sizable chunk of liquid funds in his retirement account that the couple had used to provide the initial donation to the family foundation. Noah and Barbara's wills each stipulated that a sizable amount would be donated to the foundation upon their deaths as well. The Steins were thrilled at the legacy they would leave for the family and the opportunity the foundation presented for the family to work together in a positive and constructive way for the betterment of the lives of those who were less fortunate.

Sharon drafted an outline for the meeting, keeping in mind the guidance from Noah and Barbara about the potential emotional and psychological potholes that lurked below the surface between the kids. As Jane Hewson, a well-known business strategist and executive coach with Beresford Partners, LLC, told me during an interview on my radio show, for a Money Talk to succeed, everyone has to accept the various ways of looking at money and different individual styles. Daniel and Janis were a little more relaxed about money, probably because they were financially more secure and had stable and predictable incomes. Sandra and Denise were less so, as they were dealing with different economic realities and often struggled with money fears. Barbara and Noah told Sharon about the sibling rivalry between the two oldest girls. Noah admitted to a tendency to favor his son, Daniel, and to baby the youngest, Denise. Barbara and Noah knew that emotional issues and patterns of behavior would not simply evaporate, but they thought that if they and Sharon were well prepared and had rehearsed the meeting, they could focus on achieving the outcome they wanted and minimize any "noise" that might interfere.

It is critical that you rehearse what you plan to say in any difficult conversation, whether professional or personal. When you are trying to be commanding and persuasive, there are few things worse than starting the conversation without being prepared. If you have not done your homework, constructed an outline of "talking points," and determined an agenda and objectives, you will be more likely to be at a loss for words, be physically tense, and use the wrong tone and body language. And when you are focusing only on what you want to accomplish in the conversation, the Money Talk will not go well. Jane Hewson told me that a vital part of rehearsal is to place yourself in the shoes of the person who is receiving the information. Think about what is important to that person and how to best engage him in a way that will ensure that he listens. Consider practicing in front of a mirror so that you can watch your facial expressions as well as listen to your language. Alternatively, ask a friend to observe and give feedback on your body language and how you say things, both in words and in tone.

Once Barbara and Noah had signed off on Sharon's agenda, they reviewed it several times to make sure they were comfortable with the content and flow of the talk. The couple had been part of a Money Talk with Barbara's parents and her two brothers a few years earlier that had not gone well, at least in part because her parents hadn't prepared what they wanted to say. Barbara and Noah discussed what they wanted to say, tweaked the language they would use, and practiced the talk a number of times in front of each other, deciding along the way who would be responsible for each section.

While rehearsal is vital, it is also important to realize that you need to remain flexible so that you can listen effectively and react accordingly. Barbara and Noah knew that their kids could react in any number of ways. The couple had to be prepared for negative responses. They could not control their kids' reactions, but they could anticipate them and be emotionally ready for them. Like Robin Williams, a master of improvisation, Barbara and Noah knew that they had to be ready to set their scripts aside and react spontaneously if need be. While the outline gave them a sense of confidence, they didn't want to appear too much in control. Michael Pruitt, an ordained Presbyterian minister who was a marketing professional before he joined the clergy, addressed that issue in another interview on my radio show. He warned that if you come into the Money Talk with too tight a set of outcomes, someone in the room will sense that you are dictating the conversation, as opposed to having an open discussion. To send a message of openness and encourage dialogue, Michael recommended keeping your hands in an open position when making your points. He stressed that body position can set the tone and make a huge difference in the delivery of a message.

The Steins's advisor, Sharon, had supervised many Money Talks among family members and had a number of pointers to give Barbara and Noah. She warned that in many difficult conversations, emotions take over and people become angry or silent, no matter what the other parties do to try to avoid that outcome. In many of these cases, people are listening to an internal dialogue rather than the actual conversation that is taking place, and, as a result, the conversation begins to break down. Sharon advised Barbara and Noah to remain focused on their motives, no matter what happened. She asked them to think about how they would behave if they really wanted these results and model their actual behavior based on that vision.

From their past experience with Barbara's parents and her brothers, Barbara and Noah knew of a number of mistakes they wanted to avoid in their own Money Talk. Holly Weeks, author of *Failure to Communicate: How Conversations Go Wrong and What You Can Do to Right Them*, wrote that there are some common mistakes that everyone can avoid. First, do not permit yourself to fall into a combat mentality that requires a winner and a loser. If there is a toxic environment, try not to lash out or shut down out of fear, anger, embarrassment, defensiveness, or any other unpleasant feeling. Make sure you do not attempt to oversimplify what you want to address. If the issue was not complicated, it probably would not be so hard to talk about. Finally, do not let emotions lead you to lose sight of your goals and the preferred outcome.

Barbara and Noah already had their own agenda that they had developed with Sharon. But they decided that they would prepare a "public" agenda that they would share with all their children at the meeting. They thought, and Sharon agreed, that having something on paper would help everyone stay focused on the practical items. They also knew that Denise had an annoying habit of interrupting and asking questions when others were talking. The Steins felt that if they had a formal agenda, Denise would realize that all the issues she cared about would be addressed and, as an item on the agenda, that she would have the opportunity to ask questions, hopefully without interrupting.

Along with flagging the emotional and psychological backstory of each individual in the family, having an agenda satisfied the meaty and practical side of preparing for the Money Talk. And, providing a detailed agenda to each person in the room would help to guide the family through all the important points step by step. That is what Noah and Barbara decided to do. They thought it would help to keep the conversation on track, especially as everyone was well aware of Denise's horrible habit, which could quickly break down the flow of the meeting and disrupt their progress toward the goals and objectives they had established. Here is a simplified version of the agenda they prepared:

1. Introduction by Barbara and Noah—why we are here and what our mission and goals are
2. Overview of the estate plan by Barbara and Noah—the pieces of the puzzle
   a. Real estate and investment assets
   b. Personal assets
   c. Wills
   d. Trusts
   e. Family LLC
   f. Family foundation
3. Details of the estate plan by Sharon (with PowerPoint and diagrams)
   a. Real estate and other investment assets
   b. Personal assets
   c. Wills
   d. Trusts
   e. Family LLC
   f. Family foundation
4. Brief break
5. Questions, concerns, and reactions to the estate plan— moderated by Sharon
   a. Daniel
   b. Sandra
   c. Janis
   d. Denise
6. Initial discussion of issues raised—moderated by Sharon
7. Open items to address at the next and subsequent meetings— execution of recommended changes, unresolved estate plan issues, family values, family mission statement, family governance, foundation philanthropy, delegation of responsibilities, education initiatives and personal development.
8. Scheduling and items on the agenda for the next family meeting and appointment of the leader of the next meeting

With all this preparation done, Barbara and Noah knew that they had one last thing to work on before the Money Talk. They needed to make sure that they approached it with a positive attitude. If you think something is going to be horribly difficult, it probably will be. If you truly believe that whatever happens, some good will come of it, that is more likely to be the case. Barbara and Noah knew that if they set aside their fears and trepidations, and believed that wonderful things would come out of the family having this conversation, they would have a higher probability of a successful outcome.

Early on the third day of their vacation, Noah drove to the Cabo San Lucas International Airport to pick up Sharon. Noah and Barbara had worked with her for nearly a decade, and the couple had complete trust in her ability to navigate and lead the upcoming Money Talk. Sharon had done a great deal of her own planning for the meeting. Dr. Hendrie Weisinger, clinical/organizational psychologist and author of *The Genius of Instinct: Reclaim Mother Nature's Tools for Enhancing Your Health, Happiness, Family, and Work*, describes instinctual tools that can be used to your advantage—including beauty, caregiving, cooperation, and curiosity. Being familiar with the theory, Sharon made sure to consider the tools in planning and conducting the meeting.

Sharon decided against holding the meeting in one of the family's hotel rooms, in a restaurant, or poolside because of potential distractions and lack of privacy. Instead, she called the resort and arranged for the family to use a small conference room reserved for business meetings.

When she arrived at the resort, she immediately inspected the conference room. She requested that the rectangular table be replaced with a round one. Roundtable seating always feels more intimate and less hierarchical, and often promotes more open dialogue. The conference room had a floor-to-ceiling window that looked out onto the Sea of Cortez and the Pacific Ocean. Sharon was thrilled that the room had natural light and that with the windows open, you could hear the sound of waves breaking on the shore. She thought both would add to a relaxed but focused environment.

However, she made sure the blinds could be drawn so that she could darken the room for her PowerPoint presentation, and she received instructions on how to turn up the air conditioning if the room got too warm.

Next, Sharon checked on the audiovisual equipment and confirmed that it worked with her laptop. She knew that when moderating family financial meetings, it was important to deliver a presentation that was interesting and creative. That engages everyone's curiosity and helps keep people engaged. She knew that some of the instruments that Barbara and Noah had created, such as the generation-skipping trusts and the family LLC, were best described using flowcharts to illustrate the flow of the assets and the various parties to the instruments. But she also knew that too many visuals could be distracting. When it came time to discuss the roles each person might play and to elicit responses from the participants, she planned to focus on the conversation rather than on any slides.

Sharon had also made arrangements to have pads and pens available so that each of the Steins would be able to take notes during the meeting.

Sharon had a brief chat with Barbara and Noah before the meeting to review a few strategies she thought might be helpful. She counseled them to watch for signs that the kids were feeling threatened or that the conversation was about to break down. She suggested that if the kids started talking over one another, raised their voices, and became agitated, or if one of them began to disengage and feel threatened, Barbara and Noah should step in to restore the feeling of safety, mutual purpose, and respect.

The Money Talk was scheduled to begin at 10 a.m. Sharon thought the conversation would last at least three hours, so she arranged to have lunch brought in. She called the business services department and ordered a variety of sandwiches and salads as well as coffee, tea, and bottles of water. Though Sharon was dressed in a stunning St. John business suit and Ferragamo heels, she told Noah and Barbara to have the family dress comfortably and casually.

The kids all arrived on time. There was a bit of anxiety and stress in the air, as no one was sure what to expect. Barbara and

Noah tried to lighten up the atmosphere with small talk, but they knew that the only thing that would dissipate the tension was to begin the talk. The six members of the Stein family took seats around the table, with Barbara and Noah sitting separately in an effort to avoid any sense of parental dominance. To ensure that the Money Talk would not be interrupted and that everyone would pay undivided attention, Noah asked that all cell phones and other technology be turned off and placed in a basket that Sharon had obtained for just this purpose. Barbara then explained that she and Noah would do most of the initial talking, but that Sharon would describe the estate plan in detail with a PowerPoint presentation and answer any questions. Noah handed out the agenda for the meeting, but he made it clear that this was only a rough outline of what they wanted to cover. He encouraged the kids to be open, ask questions, and make suggestions. Barbara, who tended to get anxious when there was the potential for family conflict, made sure to breathe slowly and deeply and center herself. She understood the importance of remaining calm and centered, as it would help the kids stay calm and centered, too.

Noah began by explaining that he wanted to say a few things out loud: that he and Barbara loved and respected each other and each member of the family deeply; that he believed, after having spoken to each kid in private, that everyone shared the goal of making sure that Noah and Barbara's legacy, in terms of both money and values, would be passed on to the next generation; and that he apologized for the lack of communication in the past concerning the family finances and Barbara's health. The goal today was to begin a new chapter by fostering more open communication and dialogue.

It took Noah and Barbara about an hour to introduce and describe the estate plan in general terms and another 15 minutes for Sharon to flip through the PowerPoint slides. Sharon made sure that her presentation and explanation of the details were straightforward and understandable. She avoided excessive legalese and the highly technical traps that many advisors fall into, which often confuse the audience and create more questions than answers. Throughout that time, the couple scanned the kids' body language.

Daniel was quite attentive during the presentation, listening carefully to Noah and Barbara, focusing on Sharon's slides, and actively taking notes. Sandra, while not taking as many notes as Daniel, seemed to be giving her full attention to her parents. During Sharon's presentation, however, she started fiddling with her pen, despite seeming to maintain eye contact. Noah thought that meant she was getting bored. Janis crossed her arms when the talk turned to the family foundation, and Barbara worried that this meant she was unhappy with the idea of having to work together with her siblings. Denise looked away quite often while Noah and Barbara were talking, particularly when the subject of wills was mentioned. Barbara knew that Denise was having a hard time dealing with the consequences of the cancer diagnosis and the reason for having the Money Talk sooner rather than later. By the time Sharon's presentation came around, Denise had begun to tilt her head, which Noah took as a sign that she had zoned out.

At the end of her presentation, Sharon suggested that everyone take a bathroom and coffee break. Denise was first out the door, followed closely by her sisters. Daniel sat for a few moments longer, finishing jotting down some notes.

When everyone came back to the room, Noah and Barbara said that they would like to hear from each of the kids in turn with questions, comments, or concerns. Drawing on the work of Douglas Stone, Bruce Patton, Sheila Heen, and Roger Fisher, who wrote *Difficult Conversations: How to Discuss What Matters Most*, Sharon had coached Noah and Barbara on the four steps to make sure this question period went well: inquiry, acknowledgment, advocacy, and problem solving.

Asking each of the kids for his or her point of view was the inquiry stage. Barbara and Noah tried to really listen to what each child was saying and, equally important, what he or she was not saying. They let each child talk, without interrupting, until he or she was finished. They leaned forward when the kids were speaking, signaling that they were not just hearing what was said, but were interested in it as well. After each child spoke, Barbara or Noah paraphrased what had been said to acknowledge that they had received the messages and to remind the children that it was safe to share their thoughts. Barbara, Noah, and Sharon took notes on all the issues raised.

Once they were sure that everyone had had his or her say and had expressed any concerns, Noah, Barbara, and Sharon addressed these concerns in what could be called the advocacy step in the discussion. The couple tried to let the kids see issues from their perspective, gently pointed out what they might have missed, and tried to help clarify their position without minimizing their kids' concerns.

After addressing the issues the kids had expressed, Noah and Barbara tried to begin building solutions and solving any problems by asking what the kids thought would work.

Daniel expressed his concern over the choice of trustees and the power that they would have over the family members during the life of the generation-skipping trust. The trust was domiciled in Delaware and, as a result, avoided the rule against perpetuities. Therefore, the trust could be in existence for a very long time. Although Daniel liked the bank and the advisor associated with the account, as well as the family lawyer who served as cotrustee, he was worried that the kids would always be at the mercy of the trustees at the bank and the law firm.

After some discussion, Barbara and Noah asked Sharon to ensure that the attorney would design the trust with some flexibility so that the kids would have the power to replace a trustee under certain conditions if the relationship was unsatisfactory. And they agreed that the kids would be allowed to see the documents related to the estate plan so that they could review them with their own advisors and develop questions that could be addressed at the next family meeting.

When her time to speak came, Sandra crossed her arms and said she wanted to know why only Daniel and Janis were assigned executive positions in the foundation. She felt that her parents were expressing their bias and displeasure over her decision to stay home and raise her children when her first child was born a decade ago. Sandra explained that she actually wanted to return to work and thought that working in the foundation could provide her with meaningful work experience and serve as a way to update her résumé.

Barbara and Noah were surprised by Sandra's concern. Instantly they realized that while they had correctly assumed that Denise had no interest in foundation management, they had not realized that Sandra might welcome the opportunity to gain business experience. Barbara and Noah immediately agreed with Sandra. They apologized for the oversight and explained that they had not intended it as a slight. They also apologized for anything they had said or done that might have led Sandra to think they were not as proud of her as they were of Daniel, Janis, and Denise. Sharon interjected that she and the attorney could work together during the week following the meeting to amend the foundation document to provide for a three-person management team. Sandra uncrossed her arms and seemed to relax.

Janis, who had been looking away from Sandra while she spoke her piece, said she wanted to know why Sandra and Denise, who had received monies from the parents throughout the years, would get the same amount as she and Daniel, who had not received monetary support. Sandra immediately recrossed her arms. Barbara concentrated on her breathing and her body language in response. Noah had pointed out to Barbara beforehand that she instinctively folded her arms across her chest and scowled whenever Janis said anything about the monies that the parents had given to Sandra and Denise. Noah looked on approvingly as he saw Barbara instead lean forward and listen closely to Janis. Daniel said nothing, but he put his pen down, leaned back in his chair, and looked intently at Noah and Barbara. Denise stared at a painting on the wall, looking as if she wished she could be anywhere else.

It was now time for Barbara and Noah to articulate their position in a calm and thoughtful way. They explained that the children had had different needs throughout their lives and that the estate plan was designed to ensure that each was taken care of when the parents died. Barbara and Noah said they didn't think it was fair to penalize one child or reward another based on the lifestyle and professional career choices they made that resulted in their having disparate financial levels as adults. Having said that, they stressed that the will had a makeup provision that addressed loans that had been made to Sandra and Denise and that would have to be repaid to the estate or forgiven at their death, which would reduce the kids' inherited portion. Sharon had explained to the Steins that regardless of the age of the children, the dispensing of money was equated with love and that it was important to treat them equally at the end of the day. However, they would continue to quietly help those who were less financially able while they were alive.

Denise still had not raised any issues on her own. In an effort to make sure that her interests were addressed as well, Barbara and Noah decided to reiterate that they wanted Denise to also be involved in the foundation and suggested that she research a handful of charities and help decide which ones the foundation would support. Denise sheepishly agreed.

As Noah wrapped up the meeting, he told the kids that he and Barbara would like to have another meeting with them soon to review the changes and address any other questions or concerns. It was agreed that they would all meet in a month at another destination. Barbara said that rather than she or Noah or Sharon leading the meeting, they would like one of the kids to take charge. Daniel volunteered and, after knowing glances among the three girls, they all agreed. They also agreed to include Sharon at that meeting to help maintain a tone of impartiality and facilitate an open discussion, if necessary.

Barbara and Noah could not have been more pleased with the outcome of the Money Talk. While the situation that had prompted it was disturbing, they felt that the meeting had yielded more than just financial clarity. Family issues that had bubbled under the surface had also been raised and addressed. It felt like they were closer than before the meeting began. The Steins were convinced that all their advance planning had been well worth it. And they were certain that having Sharon, their financial advisor, help them with the meeting, both in the planning and as an effective and respected third-party moderator and educator, had been the right choice.

As of this writing, Barbara is still battling cancer. Treatments have slowed the disease sufficiently that she and Noah are looking forward to at least a couple of additional annual family vacations with their children and grandchildren.

Having a trusted advisor to help orchestrate the conversation allowed Barbara and Noah to turn a situation that could have shattered an already anxious family into an event that brought everyone closer together while resolving practical concerns. That is why, in the next chapter, I will give you a step-by-step guide to finding an advisor who is right for you and who can help you have a successful Money Talk.

Things to Think About

- Have you ever held a Money Talk before? If so, what happened?
- What do you think made your earlier Money Talks successful, or what led to their being failures?
- What are some of the concerns you have about holding Money Talks?
- If you have a need for a Money Talk, have you carefully thought through your objective or goal, the transition point, and the financial topics and issues around it? Have you tried to put them in writing to help you clarify them and communicate them at a later time?
- Are there any particular family pain points, such as longstanding sibling rivalries or differences in monetary support between children, that might make the Money Talk difficult?
- Do you have a history of communication challenges with anyone in your family? If so, what are they? What role have you played in making those conversations successful or not?

(continued)

- When you need to have an important conversation with your family, do you develop a well-thought-out plan covering what you want to say, why you want to say it, and where, when, and how you want to say it?
- Have you thought about the various evolutionary instincts and elements, such as creating a visually pleasing environment, that could help you orchestrate the conversation?
- Have you considered your motives for the Money Talk? What do you hope to achieve? What do you want for others and for the relationship? Are your goals realistic?
- Can you anticipate where you might have difficulty when talking to individual family members and thought about how to handle it? How, for example, will you deal with anger and possible resentment?
- Have you considered as part of your conversation the four steps for addressing conflict: inquiry, acknowl-edgment, advocacy, and problem solving?
- Do you have any resistance to creating a script for your Money Talk and practicing it in front of either someone else or a mirror? If you are hesitant, why? Do you rehearse other important personal or work dialogues?
- Do you have an advisor or an independent third party who can help you prepare for a Money Talk, and perhaps help lead it? If not, what other roles can your advisors play in assisting you in the Money Talk?
- If you do not have an advisor or third party to call on, is there one family member who you think would be best capable of leading a Money Talk? Why? Is there one family member who you think would be unable to lead a Money Talk? Why?

10

Ask for Help

The Roles Professionals Should Play in Your Family's Money Talk

From your confessor, lawyer and physician.
Hide not your case on no condition.
—John Harington

S am Zamansky emigrated from Poland to the United States. He came through Ellis Island with his parents and four siblings before World War II. Settling in a racially and ethnically integrated neighborhood in Detroit, the family opened a candy and convenience store and lived upstairs. From an early age, Sam worked hard. He was a newspaper boy throughout his youth, then he drove a cab while he attended college and medical school. Despite having to work, he finished near the top of his class. After completing residencies at medical centers around the country, Sam established a family practice in a small town in upstate New York.

Sam had a loving 40-year marriage to his wife, Lillian, and they had two active and engaging children, David and Sarah. As the kids were growing up, the Zamanskys spent many wonderful winter vacations at a Palm Beach, Florida, condominium they had purchased as a respite from the cold and snow. The couple hoped it would become their retirement home one day when Sam was ready to give up his practice.

Unfortunately, the couple's plans changed the year Lillian celebrated her sixty-seventh birthday. She was diagnosed with an advanced case of colon cancer. After a two-year struggle to contain the disease, which ultimately spread to her liver, Lillian died. At the time of her death, the 72-year-old Sam was still working 60 hours a week caring for his patients. The shock of Lillian's death prompted him to retire earlier than he had originally planned in order to try to live some of the retirement dream they had hoped for. Three years after losing Lillian, Sam sold his share of the practice to his two partners and moved to Florida. At 75, he planned an encore career of playing golf and bridge.

Four years after settling in, Sam met Lisa, an attractive and intelligent woman 15 years his junior. Lisa, who had previously been married and divorced twice, vigorously pursued Sam. He was smitten by Lisa's charm, her flair for socializing, and her still radiant good looks. It was not long before Lisa gave up her own rental and moved in with Sam.

David and Sarah tried to subtly voice their concerns about Lisa's intent and the risks associated with the relationship. Sam would hear none of it. He was focused on putting his grief behind him and beginning a new life with the enthusiastic and lively Lisa. David and Sarah asked Sam if he had drafted a new will since their mother's death and had executed a durable power of attorney and a living will. Sam assured them that everything had been taken care of, and that there was no need to worry. Neither was true.

David and Sarah later discovered that Sam's power of attorney and will hadn't been updated since Lillian's death. Also, Sam actually had no living will or medical healthcare proxy with a designated agent to represent him. The children had assumed that, despite the shock of losing his wife and his advancing years, their father was on top of his game. He had always been savvy financially, but very private, particularly about his finances. Over the years, Sam had made it very clear that he wanted his children to know very little about his finances. He was afraid his financial success and the expectation of an inheritance would discourage their ambitions and lead them to stray from the hardworking and humble approach to life that was at the core of his values. Because of this family history, David and Sarah didn't push past Sam's reflexive rebuffs of their questioning.

Over the next seven years, the children began to suspect that their father's situation was not as rosy as he had portrayed it. But it was not until David spotted an alarming trend in Sam's IRA accounts that a warning bell went off. David, a successful financial advisor with a prominent institution, had served as the broker on the IRA accounts for many years. Suddenly he noticed that his father had been making much larger withdrawals than usual from the IRAs. After discussing the situation with Sarah, the two siblings agreed that it was time to pay a surprise visit to their father in Florida.

During the week David and Sarah were in Palm Beach, David spent a great deal of time with Sam looking through his papers and statements, and Sarah spent her time observing her father's behavior and daily activities. What the children discovered was distressing. Sam was definitely aging, and was not as type A as he had once been. He was giving in to financial requests from the beautiful younger woman in his life, and Lisa appeared to be taking advantage of his mellowing and smitten condition. She had placed her name, apparently with Sam's "approval," on all his cash accounts, as co-owner with signature rights, and had been systematically spending large sums of money on herself, her two sisters, and her three nieces. It was Lisa who had been orchestrating the larger distributions from the retirement accounts, getting Sam's signature on the withdrawal papers without his seeming to fully understand what was happening. Within seven years, Lisa had burned through almost a million dollars of Sam's hard-earned money.

Once David and Sarah realized the extent of the damage, they considered taking legal action against Lisa. But when they realized how emotionally difficult and costly the legal process would be, they decided to make the needed changes in Sam's legal and financial life and just move on.

When David told me this story, one of the first things he said was that he knew it could have been avoided. As a financial professional himself, David knew that if, after Lillian's death, his father had hired an advisory team and created a plan to protect his assets, he would have had people on board to monitor the family finances, and Lisa would never have been successful in emptying the accounts. David said that he and Sarah blamed themselves for being too busy and distracted with their own lives to see the physical and emotional changes in Sam. The death of their mom had been traumatic for him. He was a much more dependent and fragile individual with a need to accommodate and please the new female influence in his life. They also blamed themselves for not being forceful and persuasive enough when Sam and Lisa first got together.

David explained that his parents had never liked to pay professional advisory fees. That was one reason he was the broker on the IRA account. David said that this was a typical attitude among Sam's group of doctor friends. Many of them felt that they could handle their own investments. David recalled that one of them actually bragged about drafting a will using templates he'd found online. Sam's decision not to engage his lawyer and his accountant after his wife's death to put the right instruments and team in place was a costly one.

Advisors are necessary when money is at stake. Individuals and families with assets need to engage professionals. If they do not, they run a much higher risk of losing money and experiencing a failed transfer of family wealth. Luckily, more and more people are beginning to understand the benefits of working with advisors and having a team of people they can rely on. According to a 2012 Northstar/Sullivan study that surveyed 1,290 individual investors with investable assets of at least $100,000, 64 percent currently work with a financial advisor. Of these, 43 percent are very satisfied with their firm and 51 percent are very satisfied with their individual advisor.

Despite the positive feelings of those who do retain advisors, many people remain reluctant to turn to a financial or legal advisor for help. There is no single reason why. Sometimes, as in the case of Sam Zamansky, they are reluctant to pay fees. Some people think they do not need advisors and can do the necessary work on their own. Many of these people have been successful in their own professions or careers and believe that their intelligence and expertise in one field gives them the knowledge and wisdom they need to do their own financial planning. Just because someone has been a successful corporate CFO does not mean that she has the skills needed to develop a financial and estate plan for her own family. Expertise in one field does not necessarily translate into expertise in another. Those within professions know this. A dermatologist would not think of treating his wife's heart condition. He would turn to a cardiologist. An attorney who serves as a corporate counsel to a multinational company would never agree to represent her son in the purchase of a home. Yet individuals who have been successful at earning money often feel that they have all the expertise needed to protect, grow, and pass along that money. Unfortunately, those who try to do so without professional financial guidance do not realize the potential consequences for their loved ones if the family does not get the proper counsel.

Even when individuals and families know they need help, the task of identifying the type of help needed and selecting someone can seem so overwhelming and difficult that they avoid and postpone it, often until it is too late. Do you need a Certified Financial Planner or a Personal Financial Specialist? Do you need an investment advisor or a Certified Investment Management Analyst? And these are just some of the financial advisor options. Once you have selected the type of professional in any given discipline that you need, the list of how many other such professionals you might need becomes daunting too. Do you need an estate planning and tax attorney? Do you need a tax or business accountant? How about a business valuation professional? Should a social worker or psychologist be part of the team?

It is no wonder that so many otherwise intelligent individuals with a sense of urgency procrastinate when it comes to choosing their professional team. In many cases, by the time they finally seek help, it is too late—someone has died without a current will, suffered through a divorce without a plan for financial security, or lost money because of a financial scam or a risky investment that went bad. I see this all too frequently. Many families who come into my office are there for help in untangling financial problems that were created because they either didn't have a professional advisory team or had the wrong players.

My goal in this chapter is to help you decipher and work your way through the world of professional advisors. Having, I hope, convinced you of the vital need to have Money Talks, I do not want the chances that those talks and your financial life will succeed put at risk because you did not have the right professional team in place. That is why in this chapter we will go through why you need an advisory team, when it is necessary to bring your team in, whom you need on your team, what to look for in an advisor, how to find and evaluate candidates, what questions to ask candidates, and how to make sure your professionals communicate with one another and work as a team on your behalf. I will also give you the tools to evaluate how your advisors are doing for you and your family. While I will be writing about financial advisors, the same template can be used in your search for any type of professional advisor.

The world is becoming increasingly complex in every aspect of our lives, from cultural, economic, and geopolitical to psychological, emotional, familial, and medical areas. Why do we think that our financial, legal, and tax matters, with their intersecting family dynamics and complicated relationships, are an exception to this complexity? Consider all the options that you need to evaluate and reevaluate throughout every transition in your life: cash flow, investments, taxes, insurance, estate and legacy planning, retirement plans, legal issues, and business decisions. Setting aside the question of whether you have the necessary knowledge, when you have a full-time job, where can you find the necessary time to carefully assess all these decisions you face and figure out how each of these ever-changing choices impacts you and the members of your family? Realistically, you do not have the time.

Managing this complexity requires the assistance of knowledgeable and experienced professionals who can help you set financial and estate-planning goals and priorities that are right for you and your family. Then they can recommend the specific steps to be taken to reach those goals. Of course, it remains up to you to decide whether you want to follow their advice.

I have found that financial and estate-planning challenges are even more complex in families in which the first generation born in the United States must deal with the differences between their parents' immigrant money values and their more assimilated ones. Advisors can be particularly helpful in communicating and negotiating the differences.

This was certainly the case with Vinod and Ila Gupta, a couple from a suburb of Mumbai. Married in their early twenties, the Guptas both finished medical school in India and moved to Atlanta. They came with little money in their pockets, but with a great deal of intelligence and an extraordinary determination to succeed. Both Vinod and Ila took their medical licensing exams in Georgia, finished their residencies, and began their medical careers in a suburb of Atlanta. Vinod was a urologist, and Ila was a gynecologist.

The Guptas's pursuit of greater financial success was partly driven by a deep commitment to helping family members who remained in India. After decades of hard work at their practices, the couple invested in a number of small to midsize hotels and a string of retail stores. They then brought family members over from India to manage and staff the businesses. The Guptas were able to accumulate a fair amount of wealth. Their retirement plans were fully funded, and they had a nice nest egg of cash and fixed-income investments. Feeling that education was the key to their success, they transmitted that value to all four of their children.

Because Vinod and Ila had grown up in families without much money, they had no experience having money conversations with their own parents. As a result, they wisely relied on their accountant and their financial advisor to help them facilitate their Money Talks.

In one case, their daughter Anna wanted to qualify for a college scholarship. She yearned to be financially independent and did not want to use her parents' money to pay for her education. However, she was unable to qualify because her parents had established custodian accounts[1] in her name, and she was upset by this. The parents' trusted accountant, who was their principal advisor, interceded and helped explain to Anna that she would have plenty of opportunities to be independent. The accountant explained that because education was extremely important to her parents, they had made sure that they socked away enough money to pay for as much schooling as their children would ever need. Their goal was for each child to start his or her adult life without debt. The rest would be up to the child.

Over the years, Anna has become more understanding and appreciative of her parents' immigrant approach. Now a married physician, Anna is raising a daughter of her own who is enticed by the materialism of American culture. The six-year-old is obsessed with the latest fashion and gadgets. The third generation, as is typical, is fully assimilated.

Aside from helping to navigate financial instruments, plan for the future, and facilitate Money Talks like those the Guptas had with their daughter Anna, advisors can help with investment decisions. My experience has been that when otherwise successful individuals who lack the right knowledge and experience to make investment decisions make those decisions on their own, they suffer losses that could have been avoided with competent advice and careful thought. Often overconfidence based on other successes in life, combined with a lack of knowledge of inherent risks and an unwillingness to pay a fee, leads to financial disasters.

Whenever you are going through a transition in your life, whether it is having your first child, planning to retire, or caring for an elderly parent, you are likely to be facing new challenges. Each situation brings with it circumstances outside of your previous experiences that require you to tackle new problems and issues. Whenever I am doing something for the first time, I like to have someone beside me to guide me—sort of like a mentor—just to make sure that the outcome is successful. Whether it is learning to play golf or identifying a new investment strategy, I find it helps if I surround myself with people who know more than I do.

If you take that same approach and apply it to your life's transitions, then it makes sense to bring in your advisory team whenever you are facing or anticipating a change in your life. Why muddle through the constantly changing set of circumstances and conditions alone and without guidance? In those situations, put together a team of professionals that can help you get through this particular transition successfully.

Suppose, for example, you plan to revise your estate plan. Of course, you will make an appointment with the attorney who drafted your will. But it also makes sense to have your accountant and your financial advisors involved in the discussions, either on a conference call or at a joint meeting. Each advisor can bring his unique and valuable accounting, legal, or financial perspective and specific knowledge to the changes in your estate plans.

Ellen and Joseph Apcot were finally going to get away. For two long years they had been working as lawyers in pressure-cooker Denver law firms while jointly caring for their newborn daughter, Alice. They had tried for ten years to have a child, and as a result they did not want to leave her side for the first two years of her life. But now that she was developing nicely and they had a wonderful nanny, they finally felt comfortable about taking a few days off and having some time alone.

They decided on a long ski weekend in France as part of a European vacation. Both Ellen and Joseph loved to ski, having grown up and gone to school in Colorado, and spent numerous weekends skiing with their families and friends. In fact, they had first met as teammates on their college ski team. Aspen was where they had spent most of their winter vacations before Alice arrived.

The first day of their weekend was unusually cold, windy, and icy. Unable to see and think clearly at the end of a long ski day, they had found themselves in an unauthorized area of the mountain. They began making a final run down the mountain and were going at considerable speed when, without warning, they both hit a huge patch of ice at a very dangerous point on the mountain. They went out of control and fell off a steep cliff, landing in a bed of rock and trees. They never had a chance of survival. Their two-year-old daughter was instantly left parentless.

Ellen and Joseph both came from strong and close families, who immediately flew to Denver to sort out the will and Alice's care. What developed was a bitter custody battle between Ellen's sister Jan and Joseph's brother James. Despite their both being lawyers, Ellen and Joseph had failed to update their wills after the birth of their child. They had never chosen guardians for Alice or provided instructions regarding her care should anything ever happen to both of them.

After months in the courts, Jan was granted custody. But the emotional fallout has lasted much longer. Jan's two grown children and her husband of 20 years had to learn to integrate a two-year-old child into their lives. Jan has had to turn back the clock and become the mother of an infant. And the lack of updated wills has had the unnecessary result of causing disharmony and strained relationships among the members of Ellen and Joseph's extended family that is still present today and may never go away.

The lesson here is obvious. Once you get your estate plan in place, it is absolutely essential that you update it regularly, particularly when you are facing a transition in life. When you are working with advisors, they will make sure to urge regular reviews and updates every time you enter a new stage of your life.

Just as your medical team consists of a number of individuals— internist, cardiologist, gynecologist, dentist, pharmacist, chiropractor, and personal trainer, for example—your financial team needs to include a number of specialists. You may not need to sit down with all of them every time you meet with one of them, but you will want to know that they are available to you when you need them and that they can all work together if necessary.

The typical team of financial advisors will begin with a Certified Financial Planner and/or wealth advisor, a Certified Public Accountant, and an estate-planning attorney. Some families may eventually need to include a psychologist, social worker, or caseworker if there are serious health concerns or potentially divisive family conflicts to deal with.

The declining health of elderly family members often brings up financial as well as emotional issues and can create wedges in family relationships. A caseworker or therapist can help all the family members navigate the elder-care issues as well as deal with the psychological impact of aging parents. Adding a geriatric-care manager to your team might be exactly what you need to establish a plan for the ongoing care of an aging family member.

Perhaps a parent is contemplating retirement and needs to create a succession plan for a family business. There are psychologists and consultants who specialize in business succession planning and who have training in dealing with the emotional and psychological fallout that is often central to this major life transition. These third-party professionals work with families who own businesses to set up objective criteria for assessing individual capabilities and skill sets. They can help determine the best roles in the business for family and nonfamily members, map out the legal logistics, and provide necessary counseling concerning the psychological and emotional issues connected with the structural changes. They can be invaluable when dealing with the potentially prickly and divisive pieces of the succession plan, and can help to resolve the conflict that often arises around the change in roles that family members have to adapt to, both within and outside of the business.

Frequently, the first advisor brought onto a new team is the financial professional. That is because finances are the thread that runs through all the important life transitions, often playing a more prominent role than legal matters. As a result, the first obstacle you may face is having to decipher and analyze the various designations given to financial professionals. As a starting point, I will briefly go over the major designations.

Certified Financial Planners (CFP®) provide financial planning and advice on topics ranging from retirement planning, investments, and taxes to estate planning, employee benefits, and insurance needs. To receive a CFP certification, they need to pass college-level courses on all the topics mentioned, and then pass a two-day, 10-hour exam. CFPs must have a bachelor's degree and a minimum of three years of professional experience working with clients. CFPs will be associated with the Certified Financial Planner Board of Standards, Inc. (www.cfp.net), or the National Association of Personal Financial Advisors (www.napfa.org).

Certified Public Accountants (CPAs®) specialize in taxes. They can help clients with tax planning and preparation. They are authorized to represent clients before the Internal Revenue Service. There is a rigorous Uniform CPA® Examination that these professionals must pass. They also must be licensed by the board of accountancy in the state in which they practice. To have their licenses renewed, they must demonstrate that they have met rigorous continuing education requirements. CPAs® are associated with the American Institute of CPAs (www.aicpa.org).

CPA Personal Financial Specialists (CPA/PFS®) are CPAs who offer overall financial planning as well as advice on taxes and accounting. Before they can take the PFS exam, CPAs must already have performed a minimum of 3,000 hours of financial planning over a five-year period and be members of the American Institute of CPAs. The PFS exam covers risk management, retirement planning, investment planning, goal setting, tax planning, and estate planning. CPAs must reapply for the PFS credential every three years.

The *brokers'* role has evolved over the years. Originally they were advisors who were paid solely to trade securities on behalf of nondiscretionary clients. They would contact clients and create portfolios through individual security trades, earning commissions on those trades. In the past 10 to 15 years, however, the brokerage business model has been changing. There is a growing movement in the industry, encouraged and somewhat directed by recent government actions, toward a fee-based and discretionary rather than a commission-based model. This is believed to promote a more consultative and advisory approach to managing client monies. Under this model, brokers also function as investment advisors. As such, they are required to take an additional licensing exam and to be registered. When they operate within a brokerage firm, they are referred to as investment advisor representatives. All licensed brokers must pass FINRA (Financial Industry Regulatory Authority, the main self-regulatory organization for financial advisors) exams before they can buy or sell securities for clients, and they must pass additional state exams to meet the registration requirements in the states in which they do business or maintain clients. They must also be registered with a FINRA member, which will let you independently check their backgrounds at www.finrabrokercheck.org.

Investment advisors and *investment advisor representatives* are professionals who provide advice on securities. While a financial planner or broker may be an investment advisor, not all investment advisors are financial planners or brokers. The Securities and Exchange Commission (SEC) and most states require investment advisors who manage at least $25 million to register with them. Investment advisors who manage less than $25 million are required to register with their state's securities agency. Investment advisors must file a Form ADV with the SEC or their state. This lists the advisor's education, employment history, investment strategies, fees, complaints, and disciplinary actions. Whether you are working with an independent money manager or an advisor with a financial services firm offering advisory services, you should receive a copy of the Form ADV for each manager you use. Certain types of investment advisors are associated with the Investment Advisor Association (www.investmentadviser.org) or the National Association of Active Investment Managers (www.naaim.org). The Investment Advisor Registration Depository at www.iard.com provides links to all the state agencies and the SEC registries.

Certified Investment Management Analysts (CIMA®) provide advice on investments to high-net-worth private clients as well as institutions such as foundations, endowments, trusts, and pensions. CIMAs must have three years of professional experience as financial advisors and have passed two, two-hour exams on topics like risk management, security analysis, performance

measurement, investor policy statement, and asset allocation. CIMA candidates complete a six-month to one-year self-
study educational program and then a one-week class held
at the Wharton School, University of Pennsylvania, or the
Haas School of Business, University of California, Berkeley.
CIMAs must also adhere to a code of professional responsibility and maintain 40 hours of continuing education every two
years, including classes in ethics and professional responsibility. CIMAs are associated with the Investment Management
Consultants Association (www.imca.org).

Chartered Financial Analysts (CFA®) advise high-net-worth individuals or families who seek sophisticated investments as part of
their portfolios and value high-level individual security analysis in addition to the areas covered by those with the CIMA
designation. Typically, CFAs are employed as portfolio managers and analysts for high-net-worth and institutional clients,
including family offices, banks, mutual funds, and investment
advisory firms. CFA candidates must have at least four years
of professional experience in investments and are expected to
spend 250 hours studying for three exams covering financial
accounting, debt, equity analysis, and portfolio management.
To keep a CFA certification current, an individual must sign
an annual ethics pledge. CFAs are associated with the CFA
Institute (www.cfainstitute.org).

Certified Fund Specialists (CFS®) provide general financial planning
services, but mostly provide advice on mutual funds, buying
and selling them for clients. A CFS candidate must do a 60-hour
self-study program and pass three exams covering the use of
mutual funds, annuities, portfolio theory, dollar-cost averag-
ing, and financial planning. The course includes a final exam,
administered by FINRA, and an open-book case study. CFS professionals must sign a code of ethics before they can use the
CFS credential. To keep the CFS status, a designee must take
30 hours of continuing education once every two years. CFS
holders are associates with the Institute of Business & Finance
(www.icfs.com).

For more in-depth information on the various credentials and the organizations that issue them, visit the FINRA website at www.finra.org.

Not knowing how to find candidates to be financial advisors leads many people to pause or procrastinate on putting together a professional team. With everyone competing to manage your money—from banks and accounting firms to mutual fund families, brokerages, hedge funds, and money managers—and with so many different credentials and designations to sort through, where should you look? Confusion, fear, or a lack of agreement among family members on what professional to use can all derail the search. It can be difficult to confide the highly private affairs of your family to a stranger and to turn over confidential documents and the responsibility for sorting out your financial world.

The first place anyone would be inclined to look when choosing a professional is a licensing body or professional association. You would not go to a doctor who did not have a medical license or a surgeon who was not board certified. Unfortunately, almost anyone can call herself a financial advisor. There are no universal industry, state, or federal regulations. Luckily, as I outlined earlier, some individuals are members of professional organizations or are subject to government agencies that provide regular oversight. For example, I receive oversight from FINRA, which has professionals on its staff who regularly monitor the designations and licenses that I and other members can use and our business activity. Advisors like me who are employees of financial services companies also have compliance teams at their organizations that offer another level of oversight and have the responsibility of making sure that the firms and their employees comply with the regulations designed to protect investors. Often, skilled advisors are members of other associations or are monitored by other regulatory agencies as well. Because of the lack of one industrywide standard, it is imperative that you do your due diligence and make sure that you hire a financial advisor who has earned specific credentials, certifications, or licenses and is in good standing with reputable organizations and any regulatory "watchdog."

Of course, no credential or license provides a guarantee against fraud or incompetence. Still, these designations do ensure that you will be working with a person who has had considerable training, and has appropriate knowledge in specific areas, and is subject to ongoing continuing education requirements and professional oversight by a governing body. If that person fails to act in a professional, ethical manner, then the industry or government group responsible for his supervision will publish the complaint and, if it is serious enough, will strip the professional of that credential or license. However, it is important to remember that just having had a complaint made against a professional is not necessarily evidence of wrongdoing. You will need to look into the issue further. Frivolous complaints can be leveled, and are often settled for expendiency's sake.

Matters are a little easier when you are dealing with estate lawyers. The Estate Law Specialist Board is an attorney-run subsidiary of the National Association of Estate Planners & Councils. It is the only American Bar Association–accredited program for certification of an attorney as an Estate Planning Law Specialist (EPLS®). To obtain board-certified status, an attorney is required to practice for five or more years as an estate-planning attorney, during which period at least one-third of the attorney's practice has to be devoted to estate planning. The specialist must also have 12 or more hours of continuing legal education in estate-planning topics each year for the last three years, verification of professional liability insurance coverage, and recommendations from at least five colleagues that are not related to or within the same firm as the applicant. Finally, the attorney must pass a comprehensive exam.

Instead of focusing on professional credentials, many high-net-worth families rely on referrals from their current advisors, business associates, friends, or family members. If your most trusted advisor or a respected colleague at the office can vouch for an individual with whom she has worked for a meaningful period of time, that is someone you should consider contacting. Just make sure that you do some of your own due diligence and ensure that the advisor being recommended works with families with your particular profile. You should never assume that just because a person lives in your neighborhood or belongs to your golf club, he has the same balance sheet or financial needs as you. If you and your spouse are planning to retire and you have a complicated set of financial circumstances, an advisor working with a respected coworker who just got married may not be right for you. You would want to make sure that the advisor also had considerable experience working with retirees in your particular financial and economic situation.

Many affluent families are concerned with maintaining their privacy and confidentiality. That leads them to look for professionals outside their community and their network of friends and family members. If you are in that situation, you can use your research skills to come up with candidates. For example, you could combine the geographic and credential preferences that you are looking for and plug them into your favorite Internet search engine to get a list of names to consider. You should never base your selection of a financial advisor on Internet research alone. However, there is nothing wrong with using the Internet to develop an initial pool of candidates that you then check on with the relevant associations and interview personally.

I recently had someone contact me after searching for a financial advisor with Morgan Stanley in my county with a Certified Public Accountant designation. The client and his wife had moved to the New York area for exciting new jobs and were in search of an advisor with a specific set of criteria in mind. Securities firms establish guidelines for their compliance professionals and the advisors they supervise and often do not permit the use of the CPA designation in the advisor's bio or letterhead or on the advisor's website. However, because I was allowed to post my membership in the New Jersey CPA Association on my website, this new high-earner client contacted me and scheduled an interview.

Whether you are approaching an existing advisor, friend, family member, or business associate for potential candidates, or you are conducting an Internet search, you will want to obtain several names. I recommend that you speak with at least two or three advisors of each type before you hire one.

In general, as with any professional, you will want to know each candidate's past work experience, professional specialties, accreditations, and required licenses. You can get a lot of these basic facts from an individual or company website, a team and/or company brochure, an industry association, or a regulatory website. For example, law and accounting firms typically have extensive websites that discuss the firm's services and post the biographies of each professional. Many financial advisors have individual websites, whether or not they are associated with a large firm. However, you may want to verify that the information posted is accurate. To do that, go to the industry regulatory agencies and industry associations I wrote about earlier.

However, at the end of the day, you need to feel comfortable with each member of your team. You need to undertake the same research and due diligence when you select an advisory team as you would if you were choosing someone to physically care for your loved ones. No referral, reference, or degree can tell you whether a particular professional is the right fit for you and your family. The selection of a team often comes down to chemistry. How do you actually feel when you are sitting across from the advisor? Does this person relate well to you and your family members? Does she understand your issues and have the right mix of talent, experience, and people skills to get the job done? These questions can be answered only by a face-to-face meeting. Many advisors give initial meetings without charging a fee, so this should not cost you anything but time.

In general, when you are interviewing advisors to hire, think and act as if you were hiring this person for an important position at your company or to be a partner at your firm. Put together a list of questions and bring them with you to the interviews. In order not to waste either of your time, do your research before each meeting so that you can obtain answers to straightforward factual questions, like the person's education, employment history, and credentials. Your list should be tailored to meet the unique needs of you and your family. However, here is a general list of questions

I have developed over the years that can serve as a starting point for your own specific set of questions.

How would you describe your typical client?
A professional may have years of experience working with ultra-high-net-worth clients and helping them to set up and manage dynasty and generation-skipping trusts, but if you have more basic needs, like planning for retirement and saving for your children's college, then you want someone who has plenty of experience in those areas.

What planning services do you provide?
I have found that many times a person says that he is a financial advisor, but all he actually does is manage money. If that is all you want, then this relationship may work. But in many cases, clients are looking for a comprehensive plan that includes more than just money management. If that is the case, you will want to know whether or not the advisor is going to take a detailed look at your financial life. You will want someone who takes a holistic view and evaluates the amount and type of insurance coverage that you hold, makes sure that your estate plan is appropriate for your financial circumstances, and discusses what investments you have and what plans you should be funding for retirement. You will also want him to provide ongoing services that will give you both what you need today and what you will need down the road.

Does your planning include specific recommendations for investments or other products? If so, what kind of investments and products do you recommend, and why?

Can you recommend only a limited number of products or services to me? If so, why?

Do you provide individual security selection, or do you rely on outside money managers and focus more on asset allocation and manager selection?

Do you do research in connection with individual selection of the securities and actually make the trades?

Do you include the client in the choice of securities, or do you have discretion over the account and can trade on the client's behalf?
This line of questioning will help you determine what types of investments the advisor offers, the investment process she follows, and the type of direction you are most likely to get.

What kind of client do you work best with: one who is involved in the specific investment choices or one who is comfortable deferring to the advisor?
Some advisors work best with self-motivated, self-directed, and knowledgeable clients who like to do their own investment research and then have a discussion about the individual pieces of a portfolio before making the purchases. Other advisors prefer to work with clients who simply need someone to walk them through the process; they may need some hand-holding, but they are comfortable delegating and deferring to the advisor to make investment recommendations and choices. There is no right or wrong answer. What matters is that you find an advisor who works best with the approach you prefer.

What kind of due diligence do you and your firm conduct around investments and other products offered?
The answer to this is often a main factor in choosing one advisor or firm over another. You want to know how your advisor will investigate investments for potential fraud, mismanagement, or departing from the objectives as stated by the prospectus. Will your advisor check out the firms' balance sheets? Will he investigate the background, experience, and stability of the personnel and how their actions line up with their investment strategies? How much of your advisor's staff or his firm's staff is devoted to the due diligence process, and how often do these people conduct their reviews?

How are you paid for your services? Are you paid on commission, a flat fee, or an hourly rate?
Advisors use many different compensation structures, and I will describe them in more detail later in this chapter. For now, it is

important to note that it is not enough for you to just know whether or not an advisor earns commissions. You will want to know specifically how much she makes from the purchase of various products that she recommends or sells to you and how the fee is calculated and charged. If you know how an advisor earns her living, then you will be better able to know whether she is working in your best interest.

How do you work with clients?
You want to learn what you can expect from your advisor's team. Who will be responsible for what, what process of regular communication is in place, and how does the team advice and guidance relate to the total compensation for the portfolio management?

Will my assets be housed with an independent third-party custodian?
This is an important question if the advisor will be providing ongoing investment advice and reporting to you. Most brokerage firms serve as custodians, and many mutual fund companies utilize third parties as custodians. For example, when clients use money managers who are independent of the advisory firm as part of an open architecture platform, the assets are traded by the outside manager, but are held by a custodian, often the brokerage firm. This is the case with Morgan Stanley, where I work. The third-party custodian will send you monthly or quarterly statements that are independent of the advisor-provided report. Your transaction confirmations and account statements will be sent to you, not your advisor. You will always write your checks to the third-party custodian, rather than to the advisor, when you are purchasing investments.

What auditor do you use?
Auditors verify the existence of the assets your advisor manages. Each state has its own database to check if an auditor is licensed. You may also want to do your own due diligence of the auditor so you will feel confident in the integrity and reliability of the audited statements.

What is your track record?
If a financial advisor works with independent money managers, he will be able to provide you with the track record of the specific

money managers he uses. However, if a portfolio is managed directly by the advisor, it may be difficult for him to provide this information. He may be customizing every portfolio for each client, based on individual needs and propensity for risk. Some advisors, however, can actually provide audited numbers. In most situations, you can informally ask about the types of portfolios that the advisor manages and estimates of the returns on client portfolios that would be similar to yours. Another question you might ask is how the advisor did during the recent financial crisis or over a certain period of time.

Can I get client references?

Ideally, you will want to ask the advisor for the names and contact information of at least two longtime clients. Be aware that some firms and advisors have restrictions that keep them from releasing names. Assuming that you are able to get names, realize that you are going to be given the names of individuals who are pleased with the advisor's services. As a result, you want to ask objective rather than subjective questions. How often does the client meet or talk with the advisor? How quickly does the advisor return telephone calls? How easy is it to schedule meetings with the advisor? How proactive is the advisor in times of financial turmoil?

Do you have any questions for me?

This open-ended question is helpful because it enables you to tell how well the advisor understands you and your situation. If you are in your mid-fifties and are dealing with an elderly parent and kids returning home after college unemployed, you might expect the advisor to ask whether your parent has long-term-care insurance and what financial obligations your returning children will impose on you. The advisor might also ask questions intended to gauge your personal money concerns, worries, and values and what transition points you will need to tackle first.

Obviously competence and integrity are requirements for any advisor. You must have confidence in the person you are working with. But trust is probably even more important, since it cuts to the heart of human relationships and the heart of the fragile relationship that, for some people, exists between the financial community and the public. Given the Madoff episode and other negative news surrounding the financial services industry in recent years, it is harder than ever for some people to tackle the elephant in the room and have trust in professionals and their institutions. Furthermore, if you do not feel completely comfortable sharing some of your most personal concerns and fears with your primary advisor, then that individual's ability to help guide you successfully through all the perilous decisions along the way will be seriously compromised. That's why trust in another person, whether it's a family member, as I wrote in Chapter 3, a professional, or both, is essential if you want to be able to have a successful Money Talk.

Aside from competence, integrity, and trust, I think communication skills are the final piece of what you need in an advisor. As I have written throughout this book, communication is essential for having Money Talks and getting through different life transitions. You want an advisor who has the knowledge and skills to communicate with the various parties who will be involved while still achieving certain performance results.

Competence, integrity, trust, and communication skills were all important traits that Connie Lee and her parents needed in a financial advisor to help the family transfer wealth. Connie, a striking first-generation Chinese American, came to this country at 19 to study at a prestigious university in northern California. A talented mathematician, Connie graduated with a master's degree in engineering in the mid-1980s and was recruited by a major technology firm in Silicon Valley. It was the beginning of the technology revolution. Connie was among the many highly educated and talented youth who emigrated to the United States from Asia in search of better-paying jobs and career opportunities.

Connie was also one of a group of Asians whose families were considered "old wealth" back in Taiwan. Her aging parents, now in their seventies, had to figure out how to distribute the family assets fairly among their three children. While Connie was the only one who had settled in the United States, the transition process was still complicated by the need to know and understand the tax and estate laws of both Taiwan and the United States. Connie's parents had to select and hire a financial advisor, an accountant, and an estate attorney who knew about both countries' tax issues, but also about the culture of Chinese families. It is often difficult for Chinese to tackle wealth planning because the discussion of death is taboo in Chinese culture.

Through referrals, the Lee family found a Chinese American financial advisor with a prominent financial institution who worked with Asian families living in different countries with multiple residences. The advisor not only had the necessary sensitivity and communication skills to work with a Chinese clientele, but also had tremendous experience with and knowledge of the complicated tax and financial issues.

Over the course of the first year, the advisor was able to earn the trust of both Connie and her parents. She was able to make the family feel comfortable with her and walk them through the necessarily complicated strategies. With the help of a competent accountant and estate attorney, they created an offshore trust to deal with the financial and tax issues. The parents funded it with appropriate assets that not only would be protected in the trust but also equitably divided their overall estate.

When Connie's father died, her mother, who historically had deferred to her husband on financial decisions, became overwhelmed. Despite the equitable distribution among the children indicated in the family trust, one of Connie's sisters was angry because of some unequal financial distributions that had taken the form of gifts from the mother to her brother. The financial advisor interceded and prevented the unraveling of the carefully and thoughtfully crafted estate plan.

Fee structures vary depending on both the specific market the advisor serves and the type of work he does. For example, if you are a wealthy family seeking a lawyer or accountant with a prominent firm that represents similar families, you can expect a fee structure commensurate with those of other prominent firms. However, if you are the owner of a small, closely held business and you need a less complicated estate plan and tax return, then you are likely to be working with an attorney or accountant who has lower fixed costs and thus a lower fee structure.

The type of fee payment will also vary depending on the circumstances. Some legal and accounting firms will charge an agreed-upon "annual retainer" for ongoing work, while others will charge fees for services on an hourly or project basis. As with any service provider, you should know in advance exactly how you are being billed.

When it comes to financial advisors, there is also a wide range of options. Some financial advisors charge a flat fee. They are paid only for the advice they give, typically on an hourly basis. They generally do not earn commissions by selling financial products such as life insurance or mutual funds or take responsibility for directly managing your monies. They will typically help you select vehicles and investments where you can place your money, with no compensation tied to the investment products. Other advisors charge a fee based on the amount of assets under management. Their fee schedule may have break points, so the percentage declines as the assets hit higher dollar levels. Or, it may be a flat fee. Still other advisors charge commission fees that are transaction-driven. There are even advisors who charge based on some combination of these approaches.

I am an advocate of a fee-based approach for clients who find it suitable and when their transaction size or the number of their transactions does not favor a commission approach. I think a fee-based approach puts the advisor and the client on the same side of the table and creates a more consultative relationship. I believe this leads the advisor to have a vested interest in delivering performance, less opportunity to generate questionable transactions, and more focus on providing advice and guidance. It also gives you a clear idea of how much you will be paying for advice.

I urge you not to base your decision solely on the fee. If you are concerned about whether a particular advisor's fees are competitive with the market, then request fee quotes and speak to other people who operate in similar markets and have comparable offerings. The most important message I want to share is that the fee should not be viewed as an obstacle to creating your A team of advisors. There is plenty of talent in the advice and guidance business, so there is no shortage of excellent options. You should be able to find advisors that fit your particular needs and demographics.

Imagine how frustrating it would be if you had fabulous individual advisors, but you found out that they were not working together to deliver the best outcome for you. One or more of them may be positioning for control, unwilling to share information, or feeling threatened by the presence of other members of the team. To make sure that does not happen, you want advisors on your team who are able to check their egos at the door. Cal Feingold, a partner with the law firm of Fellig, Feingold, Edelblum, and Schwartz LLC and a guest on my radio show, stresses that it is important that all your professionals realize that they are there to serve you and your needs first, and that means collaborating on your behalf. That may require you to have open and nonthreatening conversations with the players involved. Suggest that they meet informally for breakfast or lunch if they do not know one another. Making a personal connection helps enhance the communication and breaks down any barriers that might have been building or territorial disputes that might arise in the future.

You can help team unity by clearly identifying one professional as the quarterback, or the lead manager of the group, at the beginning of the process. She should provide oversight of the process and coordinate the flow of activities. Nancy Molitar, a clinical psychologist and assistant professor of clinical psychiatry and behavioral science at Northwestern University Feinberg School of Medicine, suggests choosing as quarterback someone who is able to step back and not let her personal ego get involved in the process. She should have the ability to manage people honestly and effectively, have a calm demeanor, and know her own limitations and strengths as well as those of the other team members.

The advisor who takes the lead has the responsibility to make sure that communication is open and fluid. That person will determine what mode of communication will be used and how frequently the team will be in touch, whether by e-mail, conference call, videoconference, or a combination. The quarterback will decide which advisors should be included in each meeting or communication. The quarterback will also advise the client about when he needs to be involved in the professional team's meetings. Conflicts and territorial disputes are bound to arise, but a good team leader can minimize and resolve them before they get in the way of the client's objectives.

When I took the Certified Investment Management Analyst course, we were taught that the final step in the process was to continuously review and monitor portfolios on an ongoing basis. I think you need to bring that same ongoing evaluation to your team of advisors.

At the outset of your relationship with every advisor, establish goals for yourself and your family. Make sure you set criteria for assessing the strength and success of your advisors, how often you want to communicate, and in what form. In the M Word spirit, it is essential that you communicate these goals and criteria to your family members and your advisors. If you have diligently thought through your objectives and criteria, you will be able to evaluate whether your relationship with the advisor is working.

If you find that the relationship is not working or that you are disappointed with any element of the service or vehicles delivered, it is best to bring this to the attention of the advisor. The team, advisors, and staff have probably spent considerable time with you in establishing the relationship and creating and executing the financial plan. You are usually best served by bringing your complaint or criticism directly to the advisor in the form of a meeting, not simply through e-mails, and having a serious one-on-one conversation to try to remedy the situation. However, if you come to the conclusion that it is time to make a change, my recommendation is that you execute the "fire" graciously. Despite the issues that may now justify or require your finding a new advisor, remember that she may have served you and your family well with dedication and affection for a number of years. Perhaps your business or wealth has expanded and you have outgrown your advisor's expertise. Or maybe you have had a change in financial circumstances and no longer are able to afford or need her services. It could be that you do not think your current advisor is meeting your performance criteria or providing you with the services that you initially sought. Or perhaps your spouse was the one who had the relationship with the advisor, and, whether because of death, divorce, or a change in circumstances, he is no longer in control of the advisory relationship. Whatever the reason, if this person has been a loyal, committed, and trustworthy member of your advisory team, then I recommend that you end the relationship gracefully, without rancor, with full disclosure, and with a sense of gratitude. Your paths may well cross again, and you may need to call on her for details concerning a specific transaction. But even if that is not the case, someone who has served you to the best of her ability deserves a respectful end to the relationship.

It might be uncomfortable, but I suggest that you end the relationship with face-to-face communication, rather than through e-mail or over the telephone. This gives you a chance to fully disclose the reasons for the change and to thank the advisor for her past service to your family.

My years as a financial advisor have given me some inside insights into choosing a team of advisors.

First, look for "substance over sales" with each advisor you hire. Whether you are interviewing financial advisors, attorneys, or accountants, find out as much as you can about each one's knowledge base. You want to be sure that the advisor you choose has substantive experience and expertise with the specific types of problems and life transitions you are facing. Smooth pitches and winning smiles can be incredibly seductive. But do not let them persuade you. Take the time to evaluate the advisor and do your due diligence. Make sure the advisor takes a long-term view of the relationship. One sign of that is if the advisor will take the necessary time to create a plan for you rather than take shortcuts to strike a quick deal with you.

Second, evaluate the advisor's various team members and support staff that will be working on your case or account. Often, the professional that you carefully evaluated will pass the day-to-day tasks to a younger or less experienced person. You want to know and understand the various roles and responsibilities of each member of the advisor's team and meet them all before you make your decision. Few people realize the huge difference that support staff makes in client account administration. Without a competent staff to support the key advisors, the world's best planning can end up with frustration and unmet expectations.

Third, consider the firm and the advisory and investment platform as well as the individual advisor. When you are evaluating a financial advisory team, make sure you evaluate the products and services that it can provide. I recently had the privilege of adding a new client to my roster who had been with another highly respected firm. That firm had a wide range of insurance offerings, but was short on the particular investment options that this client needed for retirement income. After careful thought and much rumination, he made the decision to change relationships and fully disclosed the reason to his advisor. The former advisor completely understood and graciously cooperated with the transfer of the accounts.

Not all firms are created equal in terms of product offerings or services. Some firms underwrite the products they offer, so they are proprietary in nature. Other firms offer the client access to an open architecture of investment choices or a combination of both. In the open architecture, the advisor, and thus the client, is permitted to build the portfolio from the "best in breed" investments. This translates into accessing the investment talent available at many different global investment firms. That, in my view, is the best approach for clients who are seeking investment excellence.

Fourth, do not obsess over track records. I know it can be comforting to reach for what appears to be an objective measurement when comparing advisor candidates. But comparing track records can be like comparing apples and oranges. Many advisors have different investment strategies, so comparing performance can be frustrating and also yield erroneous results. It is always best to know what the benchmarks or indexes are relative to performance when embarking on the exercise. In addition, financial advisors can have different skillsets and business models because of their different education and experience. This often translates into advisors offering different products and services. For example, an advisor who works largely with young, affluent individuals with a high tolerance for risk may have an impressive track record at outpacing market averages during bullish market cycles. However, she may not be able to evaluate clients' company benefits or address their planning concerns as they evolve. She also may not have an understanding of all the hedging strategies that can be useful in reducing volatility. Compare this advisor to another advisor with more experience who is part of a team, who works largely with older affluent individuals approaching or already in retirement, and who is involved with estate planning, insurance needs, and real estate mortgages as well as investments. He may be constructing portfolios with sophisticated asset allocation strategies and delivering solid returns based on his clients' more moderate risk profiles, while staying on track with all his clients' various planning needs.

I have found that most clients are best served by financial advisors and teams that are able to take a holistic approach to the client's financial situation and have access to independent investment options and a number of financial advisory instruments and services. Furthermore, it is important to remember that someone who takes all of your unique family needs into account is probably not going to be able to be the same person who is doing daily trading and delivering returns for you as a "money manager" who does not deal directly with the client. You want someone who has a competitive track record through her product offerings. But, more important, you also want advisors who listen, understand your particular set of circumstances, and are able to solve problems and bring ideas and solutions to you and your family. How much risk you can assume from an investment point of view is a basic assessment. As the advisor digs deeper, other issues should surface. Is there additional risk based on a medical condition or the health of your business or industry that should be factored in? Are there special lifestyle plans, such as the purchase of another home, an ailing parent, the return home of an adult child, or a change of careers, that need to be considered as part of your problem solving? Do you have a special desire to be of service or to inculcate a sense of philanthropy in your family? It is only an advisor who looks at you and your family as complex, unique human beings, rather than just a set of numbers, who can provide the kind of service you need and deserve.

Fifth and finally, I want to remind you that communication is the key. It is the secret ingredient for establishing a successful working relationship with your advisor and managing financial transitions with your family members. Personal chemistry is very important, but unless an advisor has strong communication skills, he will not be able to quarterback your team effectively or ensure that your Money Talks succeed.

Things to Think About

- Do you have a team of advisors who help you with your taxes, estate planning, and financial plan?
- If you do not have a team, what professionals do you think you need in order to create the right team?
- If you do have a team and you want to replace one or more members, which are they? Why are you not satisfied with them? What traits would you look for in replacement members that the current members of your team lack?
- Does your team have the right combination of licenses, credentials, experience, and knowledge in the areas you need?
- Does your team have the necessary chemistry with you and your family, as well as the communication skills you are looking for?
- Are you prepared to do all the work that needs to be done to find the right advisor or team of advisors? If not, why not? If you are not prepared to conduct the search, is there another member of your family who can do it? Is another member of your professional team capable of doing the initial search for you?

(continued)

- What situations are facing your family that you need to address in interviewing candidate advisors?
- Is there anything unique about your family that should be discussed with potential team members? Is there a special expertise you might need in order to deal with current or future issues?
- Do any members of your existing advisory team appear to have the ability to act as quarterback of your team? If not, do any of the advisors you are interviewing appear to have the ability to act as quarterback of your team?

11

Practice Makes Perfect

Planning for Successful Money Talks over the Long Term

The world's a stage and most of us are desperately unrehearsed.
—Sean O'Casey

In his bestselling book *Outliers*, Malcolm Gladwell explores the various factors that contribute to success. He came away from his research with the "10,000-hour rule." Gladwell believes that what separates the truly successful, the outliers, from the rest of us is that they have had, either by design or by default, the opportunity to practice specific tasks for more than 10,000 hours. For example, he explains how the Beatles, by performing frequently in Hamburg, Germany, over the course of four years, amassed more than 10,000 hours of practice before they hit it big, and how, by gaining access to a high school computer at the age of 13, Bill Gates was able to put in more than 10,000 hours of programming by a very early age. I do not think you will need to devote 10,000 hours to Money Talks in the course of your life. However, I expect you will have ample opportunities to practice your financial communication skills and become a more skilled Money Talker.

You can and should be having talks as often as needed concerning the financial issues you are facing as you experience or, even better, anticipate each of life's transitions: births, marriage, divorce, remarriage, blending families, changes in careers and financial circumstances, the return of adult children to the home, declining health status, aging family members, retirement, transferring wealth, preparing heirs, and death.

But Money Talks need not always be focused on large, life-altering events. In fact, it would be wonderful if you and your immediate family, if not your extended family, began having regular Money Talks weekly or monthly to address more everyday financial issues that arise: the increasing cost of groceries and gas and its effect on the budget, the impact that a shuffle in family duties is having on cash flow, or the local charity event that needs support in the form of both money and time.

What really makes these conversations so difficult but necessary to have on a regular basis is what is occurring beyond the financial pressures you feel that are associated with life transitions and mundane daily money tasks. It is the constant bombardment, in a 24-hours-a-day, seven-days-a-week news environment, of national and global events and structural and technological changes that have a serious impact on your life, but over which you have no control. In the world that challenges you daily, geopolitics, the economy, and the job markets are uncertain. All of life's decisions seem more daunting than ever before. And everyone seems to be affected. Even young people today are facing challenges that have not been seen since the Great Depression and that most of their parents never experienced as youths: mountains of debt and limited choices concerning their future. All of these factors can be overwhelming to family members, heighten emotions and fears, and increase the need for more open dialogue about the topic of money.

However, having Money Talks deeply challenges our natural instinct to avoid topics that are difficult. Money Talks can stir up those old family dynamics such as control over money, trust, sibling rivalries, and anxieties related to changes within the family finances or structure. Fear of conflict can lead to inertia. And inertia, when applied to the need for financial communication, can lead to a loss of money and relationships, as I have described throughout this book. Remember, conflict is okay, and disagreements can be healthy. It is part of the problem-solving process. What matters is that you address it, solve it in a healthy manner, and move beyond it in a way that brings your family even closer.

Taking the first step toward creating a dialogue is the hardest, which for some may be a comforting piece of news. Once you overcome your fear and inertia, if you follow the guidelines I have described, you will be able to have one successful Money Talk after another. You will discover that Money Talks get less and less burdensome and can eventually become a family ritual—maybe even change the family culture. A weekly chat around the dining room table, a monthly telephone call or Skype session, or an annual discussion when everyone gathers for a holiday can strengthen your family and help maintain connections, no matter what changes have taken place in the family's dynamics.

In addition to identifying the particular transition points and issues in your lives that need to be addressed and discussed regularly, you need to understand that the conversation is never static. Once you take the first step and engage, you have to continue to repeat and reengage your family with a thoughtful strategy. However, be ready to alter and adapt to a new strategy if new information or insight has become available or if another person, such as a health or financial professional, has been included in the conversation. Whatever the time frame you have determined, it is important to figure out how to incorporate the process of having Money Talks into your own life. You will also need to determine the best ways to keep the lines of communication open so that your family will be prepared to discuss financial issues when the need arises. If you are physically separated, that could take the form of weekly phone calls or Skype sessions, as we mentioned earlier, or friendly e-mails if all the parties are comfortable with that approach. The best method, however, is informal and formal in-person visits and family gatherings where you can strengthen your relationships and make personal and meaningful connections.

Money Talks can yield "happy endings." But for that to be the outcome, communication and trust need to be part of your family culture. That means that family members need to share more openly with one another and with everyone who is critical to the conversation. They need to be able to voice their own opinions, as well as actively engage and listen to others on topics such as the family's assets and liabilities and the issues that surround the transition points. When they operate in an environment that encourages communication and the sharing of information, families can begin to form a mutually workable financial blueprint.

This is a complicated process, and I covered a lot of ground. I spent much time in Chapter 1 discussing why the money conversations are so crucial and challenging and why families should be having them now. There is a 70 percent failure rate in transferring wealth from one generation to another. Breakdowns in communication and trust are at the heart of the failed transfers and loss of money and family harmony. At the same time, there is an urgency to having the conversation. An unprecedented transfer of wealth is taking place according to the Center on Wealth and Philanthropy—more than $59 trillion between 2007 and 2061. While these talks need to take place in connection with all life transitions, money is a dirty word, a taboo subject that causes anxiety and conflict in most families.

I touched on many different reasons that make it difficult and also on some of the roadblocks to successfully having the conversation. The topics ranged from brain chemistry and generational differences to evolutionary behavior patterns and family cultural patterns. Let me briefly go over the basics of the process just to refresh your memory and help you get started.

First, you need to identify where you are in your life—what transition point you are experiencing. The answer will determine the financial topics and issues you need to address. Every transition point in life involves money. Even if you are not experiencing a specific change in your life at any given moment, you are probably planning (or avoiding planning) for one. For example, suppose your kids are in middle school, your parents are healthy and independent, and you are financially stable because your job is secure. While you have no specific transition point at hand, you should already be planning for your kids' colleges, considering your own and your parents' long-term care, and making sure you have enough money for retirement. All these issues require a Money Talk.

Once you have a good perspective on where you are in your life and the financial issues that surround that transition or planning phase, you need to outline the objectives and goals of a money conversation. You will want to think about how to address the "inner landscape." The more obvious issues are control, trust, and the roles that various family members play. But you will also need to understand the issues that are farther below the surface, such as generational and gender differences, varied individual temperaments, and even cultural issues.

While understanding is important, physically preparing for the talk is vital. You can know and understand every nuance and hidden factor and yet totally miss the boat on your Money Talk if you sit with your arms crossed and a worried look or scowl on your face. Factors like body language, tone of voice, and physical environment are essential. These factors are significantly magnified with family members who are so used to one another that there is little or no self-awareness or self-censorship. We do and say things to our loved ones that we would never do or say to strangers. You need to bring a heightened awareness to your Money Talks because the slightest gesture or simplest verbal choice can dredge up negative historical family conflicts.

You cannot let this awareness get in the way of open conversation, however. That, after all, is one of the goals. You want to be consciously aware of all the potential emotional potholes that can cause you to fail, and to have a well-crafted agenda that outlines what you want to say, but also allows others to speak their minds. Rehearsing and role playing before a Money Talk is no different from rehearsing before a wedding or a major business presentation. It does not make the moment less real. It just increases the odds that everything will go well.

Another way to increase the chances of success is to engage a dream team of advisors, such as an attorney, an accountant, and a financial advisor. In some cases, a psychologist, a caseworker, and even a family business specialist could also be helpful. Depending on the expert, he can provide valuable information, defuse tense situations, or solve a thorny problem. Do-it-yourselfers run the risk of making expensive mistakes; incomplete or wrong information can end up costing individuals more in the long run than hiring a professional to steer them right in the first place.

Then, of course, you need to repeat the process, hopefully not for 10,000 hours, but as often as needed or possible.

The Money Talk Checklist: The Five-Step Plan to Guide You Through Life's Transitions

Rather than having to go through this book from cover to cover every time you are about to have a Money Talk, I have created a checklist for you on the following pages. Make a copy of it and use it every time you are facing a Money Talk.

Step One: What Transition Are You Facing?

1. *Getting married.* To avoid problems down the road, you need to disclose your assets, liabilities, and goals; decide whether to merge or segregate your individual finances; and discuss any lifestyle compromises that may be necessary.

2. *Starting a family.* It is vital to figure out how you will provide your children with short-term and long-term financial security and education funds, and the role that insurance will play.

3. *Getting divorced.* You will have to divide marital assets while trying to preserve your financial stability and family sanity.

4. *Getting remarried.* Remarriage often involves the blending of disparate family cultures and lifestyles and requires deciding on individual and joint responsibilities and obligations.

5. *Changing jobs or shifting careers.* These changes typically mandate a fresh self-assessment of your skills and your value in the open market, an updated look at your current finances, and possibly a reevaluation of your goals.

6. *Experiencing a decline in financial circumstances.* When this happens, you are forced to reevaluate your financial state (assets and liabilities), recalculate your cash flow, reassess your lifestyle, and settle on new spending, charitable giving, and gifting patterns.

7. *Suffering from a serious illness.* You will need to assess your current and expected costs, determine your existing income resources, and integrate insurance and other instruments that can help support your care.

8. *Having to care for aging parents.* When you take over the affairs of an aging parent, you will need to determine her financial health, put together a team of financial and medical advisors,

and enact estate-planning and healthcare strategies that provide both asset protection and quality care.

9. *Having adult children return home.* "Boomerang kids" returning to the nest should prompt a calculation of the effect of the return on individual and family finances and the drafting of a plan to maintain family harmony, parental assets, and the adult child's financial and emotional independence.

10. *Preparing for retirement.* Today, this means reevaluating and possibly repositioning your portfolio and your expectations based on new economic circumstances and increased longevity.

11. *Experiencing a family death.* A death in the family forces family members to assess the effect on their own lives, both personal and financial, and to realize their own mortality. It should lead other family members to take measures to ensure that at their deaths, there will be a proper distribution of estate assets, the payment of required taxes, and the eventual settling of the estate.

12. *Preparing heirs.* If you are going to prepare your heirs and plan for a successful estate transfer, you will need to transfer family values as well as provide meaningful education and any necessary professional support.

13. *Transferring a family business.* When you transfer a family business, you have to create a plan that addresses multigenerational financial and psychological issues and the health of both the family and the business.

Step Two: Prepare the Inner Landscape

1. Consider first the obvious family issues that surround the Money Talk.

2. How has money been used as a means of control in the family? How has that affected the various relationships, and how does it continue to inform them?

3. In what ways are money and trust bound together in the family culture? How does that play out in family relationships, collectively and individually?

4. What is the historical role of each family member when it comes to money? Has someone been the caretaker while someone else

always needed to be cared for? Has a family member always been responsible and independent, whereas another was irresponsible and more dependent? And how will changes in the family and money structure affect these roles?

5. Consider the less obvious issues that play out in the Money Talk.
6. Become gender intelligent.
   a. Be aware of gender differences and accept conflict. Men and women make financial decisions very differently. These differences are not personal; they are wired and rooted in the brain and the physiology of the sexes. As a result, conflict when talking about money is highly likely.
   b. Understand and recognize the differences that are at work. Try to identify which differences are at work in your situation. Are they reflected in risk taking, the prioritizing of goals, setting a time horizon, or all three?
   c. Do not judge differences or take them personally. You may want to turn to a professional who understands gender issues to help you identify, objectify, and articulate the differences, and help negotiate a compromise.
   d. Allow for debate and space. The fight or flight instinct will lead men to want to either engage in a debate or walk away. Let them. Give them time and space.
   e. Listen, validate, and empathize. Women need to reconcile conflict through conversation. Nod and agree . . . even if you do not.
   f. Reengage in conversation. Take time off after your initial discussion, then return to a conversation dedicated to problem solving. Put yourself in the other person's shoes, and be prepared to compromise.
7. Become thinking pattern intelligent.
   a. Be aware of basic neurological engineering that can help individuals understand the role the brain plays in the economic decisions that we make every day.
   b. Understand the thinking patterns that influence decisions. Recognize the reflexive and reflective parts of your brain. This will help you control the struggle between emotion and reason when it comes to investing and making financial decisions.

c. Create a financial plan and investment strategy or policy statement, and put it in writing. If it is a financial plan, it should address your financial goals and objectives, such as retirement or educating children, as well as estate and insurance needs. Your investment strategy is part of your financial plan and needs to include the purposes of your portfolio and your expectations, time horizon, diversification strategy, rebalancing guidelines, and ongoing assessment of risk and performance.

d. Engage professionals if you do not have the skills to tackle the issues successfully. Do not feel that you have to do everything on your own. You are more likely to have a plan if you have an advisor, and having a plan or process in place is critical. Having professionals on board will help you take the time to think through decisions and maintain a rational course in the face of a crisis.

e. Communicate regularly and openly with family members and advisors. You will be more likely to stick to your plans and execute them successfully if you share them with other family members and advisors that you trust and that are integral to the plan. They can serve as a voice of reason if the reflexive part of your brain tries to take control.

f. Revisit your plans and communicate any changes. When your circumstances change, it is important that you review your documents to ensure that they still address your needs.

8. Become instinct intelligent.

a. Understand anthropologic and evolutionary behavior patterns. Humans have been hardwired to see money as an object of threat and control, and the conversation is difficult because it is tied in with sexual exchanges, which were part of money transfers in primitive societies.

b. Know the six basic instincts. Be aware of these deep human instincts: shelter seeking, care soliciting, caregiving, cooperation, beauty, and curiosity.

c. Reconnect and respond to instincts positively. Understand and be aware of all the basic instincts that are in play. Before your talk, think through each instinct and determine the best way to address it.

9. Do what you can to be a happier and more productive person. Psychologically, money is tied to our personal sense of self-esteem, self-worth, and even familial love. Having a positive outlook about yourself, your family, and your future improves your communication skills and mitigates whatever shortcomings you might have. Adopt and commit to a plan to promote positive thinking. Decide to do the following simple exercises for 21 days. If you do, you will be on the way to rewiring your brain.

    a. Jot down a daily gratitude list. Take 45 seconds every morning, when you wake up or when you get to work, to write down three things that you are grateful for.

    b. Practice meditation. Meditate for at least two minutes a day.

    c. Write in a journal each day. Once a day, spend five minutes writing about a positive experience you had over the past 24 hours.

    d. Exercise regularly. Start slowly. At a minimum, exercise three times a week for 15 minutes. Step it up to increase your endorphin level and your feeling of success.

    e. Communicate optimistically. Engage your family members in an optimistic and positive manner to help all of you solve whatever issues you are facing.

10. Become age intelligent.

    a. Understand generational differences. Realize that when you are born has a great deal to do with your money perceptions and values.

    b. Identify what's important to you. When you know and understand your own money values, you will be in a better position to express them to others.

    c. Use language that's age- and generation-appropriate and clear. When you are having money conversations, communicate in a way that the generations can understand and relate to.

11. Be knowledgeable about the family's history with money.
    a. Understand the relationship that your parents and grand-parents had with money and how that may have been passed down to you.
    b. Understand individual money personalities and family patterns.
    c. Try to determine whether or not money was used as a substitute for love or a tool for control, or whether it was used for some other not-so-obvious tactic.
12. Be culturally sensitive.
    a. Realize that social and cultural mores have been passed down through generations and have created certain attitudes about money. For example, talking about money will bring bad luck.
    b. Remember that the American national character has always been conflicted about money, as we strive for wealth and equality at the same time.
    c. Nuances about money exist between different cultures, between different generations of immigrant families, and between different parts of the country.
    d. Money politics in relationships need to be addressed, especially in couples where women equal or surpass their spouses in both education and earning power.

Step Three: Prepare the Outer Landscape

1. Before the talk.
    a. Prepare to address everything that happens before you sit down in the room for the Money Talk. This includes answers to the what, who, where, when, and how questions.
    b. Identify the catalyst for the discussion. This gets back to identifying the transition point you are experiencing in your life.
    c. Know and understand the goals and objectives that you want to achieve with the conversation. Be clear about what you want for yourself, for others, and for the relationships involved.

d. Document all your questions and concerns to help guide you through the process and ensure that you tackle each issue.

e. Work with your financial advisor, your estate attorney, and your accountant to identify what you hope to accomplish and what you think would be the ideal outcome, and to determine what topics to cover.

f. Draft an outline and agenda for the meeting with a few talking points. Rehearse your talking points in front of a mirror or with a friend. Ask for feedback on your body language and on how you say things, both in words and in tone.

g. Be prepared to approach the conversation with an understanding of the inner landscape elements that are in play: control, trust, the roles family members play, gender differences, evolutionary influences, instinctual patterns, age differences, individual attitudes, family history, and culture.

h. Think about the various ways all of those who will be participating in the Money Talk look at money and try to characterize their individual money styles.

i. Consider how you can eliminate or mitigate the "noise" created by conflicts among the various views of money and money styles.

j. Have another rehearsal, this time envisioning how all the other participants in the talk will respond to the presentation. Refine your presentation so that it is done confidently, prevents others from getting defensive, and encourages participation.

k. Do not let yourself become robotic. Prepare, but remain flexible enough to respond to the other participants. Remember that this is a conversation, not a lecture. Be aware of your typical body language and make sure it invites participation and dialogue.

l. Prepare yourself and the environment. Choose a safe, attractive, and quiet place that makes everyone feel comfortable and secure. Dress well for the meeting.

m. Prepare a public agenda to keep the conversation on track, and send it to family members in advance.

n. Once they have the agenda, suggest that your family members discuss their questions and concerns with their financial advisors in advance of the family meeting and come prepared to share them with the rest of the family.

2. During the talk.

a. Remain focused on what you really want for yourself, for others, and for the relationships, and how you should behave in order to achieve those results.

b. Always look for healthy options and opportunities to have the conversations.

c. Apologize for any role you might have played in creating family conflict around a particularly sensitive issue that might interfere with your reaching your objectives.

d. Always state your case unemotionally and support it with facts.

e. Remain aware of the inner landscape elements that are in play—control, trust, the roles family members play, gender differences, evolutionary influences, instinctual patterns, age differences, individual attitudes, family history, and culture—and tailor your approach accordingly.

f. Use appropriate language and tone. Speak in a calming tone, and use words such as *safety*, *security*, and *protection*. Let everyone know that everything discussed will remain confidential.

g. Facilitate cooperation and caring. Give every family member a role to play in the financial plan. Educate those family members who need help understanding the issues. Communicate with the family members to let them know you are working collaboratively with them to address family financial concerns.

h. Watch your attitude, and engage in a positive manner. Do not permit yourself to fall into a combat mentality that requires a winner and a loser. If there is a toxic environment, try not to lash out or shut down out of fear, anger, embarrassment, defensiveness, or any other unpleasant feeling. Make sure you do not attempt to oversimplify what you want to address. If the issues were not complicated, they probably would not be so hard to talk about. Finally, do not let emotions lead you to lose sight of your goals and the preferred outcome.

i. If you think you may need someone to lead the discussion, appoint that person in advance of the meeting. Whether or not you have a meeting facilitator, you want to make sure that everyone has an opportunity to speak.

j. As a participant, be an active listener. Look at the person speaking, and use supportive gestures as he is talking. Keep an eye on the pulse of the group as a whole and of each individual. Look for signs that the participants may need a break.

k. Build solutions. Look to solve any problems or issues that family members discussed in the meeting. Make sure everyone has an opportunity to speak, and acknowledge other points of view. Explain the reasons for your point of view, but be open to amending your plan after receiving input from family members.

Step Four: Ask for Help

1. Understand the need for a professional advisory team. It is impossible for you to manage all the complicated financial options that you continually need to evaluate and reevaluate throughout every transition in your life.

2. Know when to bring in an advisory team. Whenever you are going through a transition point in your life, it is a good idea to connect with your advisory team. At the very least, you will want to convene with your team at least once a year.

3. Decide whom your advisory team should include. Many advisory teams include a Certified Financial Planner and/or wealth advisor, a Certified Public Accountant, and an estate-planning attorney. Some families may need to include a psychologist, a social worker, or a caseworker. The transition point that you are experiencing will determine whom you choose to work with at a particular time.

4. Decide how to find advisors. Consider relying on current advisors, business associates, friends, and family members for recommendations and referrals. Whomever you choose, make sure she has the knowledge and experience you need, given your circumstances. Whether you get a referral from an advisor, a friend, a family member, or a business associate or find potential advisors through an Internet search, you will want to do your own due diligence and interview several before you hire one. Speak to at least two or three advisors of each type before you make your decision.

5. Interview each candidate. Credentials, training, professional reputation, and experience are important and serve as the fundamental basis for your decision when you are choosing advisors. To gather that information, you will want to be a savvy interviewer.

   a. Where did you go to school? What is your recent employment history?

   b. What is your background and experience?

   c. What are your credentials? What licenses do you hold?

   d. What planning services do you provide? Does your planning include specific recommendations for investments or other products? If so, what kind of investments and products do you recommend, and why?

   e. What kind of client do you work best with, one who is involved in the investment choices or one who is comfortable deferring to the advisor?

   f. What kind of due diligence does your firm conduct concerning investments and other products that you offer? What additional due diligence do you provide?

   g. How are you paid for your services? If you are speaking with an investment advisor, financial planner, or broker, you can ask if he is paid on commission, by a flat fee, at an hourly rate, or through some combination of these?

   h. What are your fees typically? Can you at some point give me an estimate based on my circumstances?

    i. For investment professionals, where will the assets be held? Will my assets be housed with an independent third-party custodian? What auditors does the advisor's firm use?

    j. Can you provide a track record based on clients who have risk profiles similar to mine?

    k. Can I get client references?

    l. Do you have any questions for me?

6. Besides expertise and experience, look for someone whom you can trust, who is honest, who demonstrates integrity, with whom you have some chemistry, and who has the communication skills needed to help with Money Talks.

7. Evaluate the various team members and support staff who will be working on your account. Learn about the firm and its advisory and investment platform.

8. Evaluate your advisors on an ongoing basis and make a change if needed, being sure to "fire" advisors graciously.

9. Look for substance over salesmanship. Superb sales skills are no replacement for experience and expertise with the types of problems and transitions you are facing.

10. Evaluate the support staff as well as the individual professional.

11. Evaluate the firm. Does it offer the kinds of products and services you need?

12. Do not obsess over track records. Remember that track records depend on strategies, and strategies vary based on clients' individual needs.

13. Look for advisors who take a holistic rather than an investment-centered approach.

14. Remember that communication skills are the most important element if you are looking for a professional to help quarterback your Money Talks.

Step Five: Repeat As Necessary

A Final Word

Even reducing almost this entire book to a checklist of a five-step plan shows you how long and arduous the journey is to overcome the taboo of the M Word and have successful Money Talks. But by picking up this book and reading it, you have done more than most people ever do. You have confronted the taboo, and, through your investment of time and the cost of the book, you have shown the initial commitment to overcoming it. You are ready. Now keep the momentum going and start planning that first Money Talk.

Epilogue

My almost decade-long exploration of the M Word has been an amazing journey. It has exponentially expanded my life experience and has stretched me further than I ever imagined I could go, creatively, intellectually, emotionally, and physically. In 2005, when I first began giving presentations at Canyon Ranch Spa about the importance of having family conversations, it was to small private groups. Initially most of my advice scratched the surface, making the connection between the unprecedented transfer of wealth across generations in this country and the need for more open dialogue about money among family members. It was informative, and it touched a strong chord with the audience, but it was mostly introductory, with some practical suggestions. Over time, however, my research, experience, and thinking led me to start digging under the surface and to examine the topic of the Money Talk on a much deeper level. I began to broaden my definition of wealth transition to include other transition points in life and to examine both the surface elements and the inner landscape of our psyches that make the conversation so difficult.

My passion for exploring the topic along with my desire to make the conversation more public led me to create and host a radio show called *The M Word*. Over the next three years, *The M Word* evolved. I addressed a range of different transitions in life that require money conversations, highlighted some of the financial issues and topics that arise at each point, and went well beyond the subject matter that I had covered in my early days at Canyon Ranch. The radio show gave me the opportunity to expand my thinking and interact with some amazing and passionate professionals and writers from an incredible array of fields. And, I was able to bring their thoughts and my own to a much larger audience than I ever dreamed I could reach in my private presentations.

The producing of the shows, the insights of my radio guests, and the ongoing experiences of Money Talks with my family and clients sparked a sense of mission in me. I felt driven to bring the message about the need to hold effective and healthy Money Talks with family members and how to do so to as many people as possible. This book is the next step in that mission.

My long M Word journey has taught me that Money Talks are extraordinarily complicated, incredibly challenging, and, for many people, terrifying. I have learned that families everywhere, regardless of their level of wealth, size, configuration, cultural background, or gender composition, are grappling with one or more of the factors we have discussed. Sometimes they are facing obvious issues, such as control, trust, or the role that family members of each generation play. Other times, they're facing subliminal issues, such as age, attitude, gender, or evolutionary or instinctual influences. I have also learned that every family is facing transitions every day; family members are either in the middle of getting through a major life situation, dealing defensively with an unexpected event that has occurred, or planning how to tackle the next change that is just around the corner.

Throughout this book, I have told a few stories of families in transition, based on my experiences working with families professionally for more than 20 years, and on my travels as a mother, wife, and community volunteer (and now writer) listening to the personal struggles of those around me. I hope that I have struck a few chords in you and that you could relate to their situations and problems. I have tried to demonstrate that while the details of families and their struggles with money are always unique, there is a sameness to them all: they all need to have Money Talks, and they usually find the prospect of such talks daunting.

As I wrote in the introduction, my family is no different. If you recall, I grew up in a home that never held Money Talks and that, in part, influenced me to pursue a career in finance, to start learning about money communications, and to put what I learned into practice, not only with my clients, but with my own spouse and children. Over the years, I have realized that talking about money requires study, knowledge, and preparation. And as with any other skill, practice and repetition both refine it and improve its chances of success. I drew on all my years of study and practice when I faced the most difficult financial conversations in my own family's history: Money Talks with my mother-in-law.

I have been happily married to my dear husband, Michael, for over 30 years. When our youngest son was three years old, we left Dallas, Texas, where we had met and married, and relocated to Bergen County, New Jersey. Other than summers at camp in Michigan and undergraduate education at the University of Michigan, I had never lived outside of Texas. Now I was living in one of the most densely populated and anxiety-producing counties in America, 15 minutes outside New York City . . . and 5 minutes from my in-laws.

My father-in-law was a sweet, unassuming, and highly intelligent man. He worked hard as a periodontist for more than 40 years while taking great care of his family and deferring to his wife on most day-to-day matters. My mother-in-law was a stylish woman with a penchant for humorous one-liners who had had a successful career as an art director on Madison Avenue before settling into marriage and raising a family. However, she also had an extremely strong and domineering personality. Her own upbringing, perhaps coupled with her need, as a woman of her day, to assert herself, led her to show little regard for the points of view or opinions of others and to feel entitled to insert herself into the daily lives and decisions of her children.

As an independent-minded professional woman of my generation, I was unwilling to cede control and decision making concerning my own family to my mother-in-law. That led to conflict. I became the recipient of regular, unsolicited, and often public criticism that was frequently expressed in a rude and insulting manner. Luckily, my mother, who had taken considerable abuse from her own mother-in-law, had trained me. For the most part, I was able to maintain my composure and treat my mother-in-law with the respect she deserved for being the mother of the wonderful man I had married and the adoring grandmother of my own two sons.

My mother-in-law had always been cared for like a princess and, because of her life circumstances, had led a life that was relatively free from tragedy. She was first catered to by her own parents, with whom she lived throughout college and her early working years until she married. From that point on and for more than 50 years, her husband, the love of her life, doted on her. He was her Prince Charming, guardian, protector, and financial provider. Her parents, whose care she was in charge of in their later years, lived well into their nineties and were healthy and independent almost right up until their deaths. Then, when all seemed to be going well, her husband fell ill and died at the age of 83 after being in and out of hospitals for a little over three months. Suddenly she had the responsibility for managing all the aspects of her life on her own. She had no experience with or knowledge about financial matters; her domain had been the home, the household, and providing tasty meals. Her husband had left only a notebook filled with a handwritten list of their assets and some statements. If anyone desperately needed help, both from her family and from financial professionals, it was my mother-in-law. And I filled the dual position as both family and a financial professional.

I mustered all my professional training and everything that I had learned over the years on how to encourage, facilitate, and lead family Money Talks. Despite our sometimes rocky past, I made a conscious effort to treat this situation as if she was just one more important client. I was fully prepared for each meeting. I had studied each problem, reviewed the related documents, and carefully thought through an agenda. I was focused on what we needed to accomplish and what I wanted to achieve, including family harmony. I rehearsed the conversations with my husband, embracing a positive attitude, strategy, and language that I thought an 80-plus-year-old woman could relate to. I was fully aware of her family history around money and the frugal and antitaxpaying values she embraced, so I knew how to frame the conversation. I came to each meeting stylishly and professionally dressed and made sure the environment in my office would be calming and pleasing. I knew that both would be vital for someone as aesthetically critical as my mother-in-law.

The family needed to work through a number of issues, none of which I can openly and fully discuss for privacy reasons. These issues required multiple meetings, some with attorneys and accountants present, others with just family members and, farther down the road, special meetings with her doctors and caseworkers. The topics ranged from probate and settling the estate to dealing with her own living conditions and deteriorating health. Getting my mother-in-law to the point where she understood and agreed was not easy. It required patience, an understanding of her particular fears and concerns, and a great deal of repeating a consistent message over many meetings and many months. Not every meeting was a success. Sometimes there was rancor and conflict. But all those involved had a chance to voice their opinions and have their feelings and ideas acknowledged. Eventually, the conflicts were resolved, and the whole family arrived where it needed to go.

The outcome was not particularly remarkable, although I must say I still take great pride in successfully moving my mother-in-law along in the process. As you have read in this book, well-planned and well-orchestrated Money Talks, often led by skilled professionals who are prepared and knowledgeable, can overcome some very difficult issues. What was remarkable and unexpected was the turnaround in my mother-in-law's opinion of me. I went from being the brunt of her criticism to one of the apples of her eye. (Her grandchildren and children always came first.) Suddenly, her son had chosen a wonderful wife, who was a terrific mother and a capable professional.

I cannot guarantee that this book will turn around your problematic family relationships. Most families have their own unique set of conflicts, independent of money issues, that are far beyond the scope of this book. However, I can state with a strong degree of certainty that with help from good advisors whom you are willing to listen to, proper planning, and skillful and repeated efforts over a period of time—probably longer than you anticipate—you will significantly increase your chances of having successful Money Talks. Learning how to overcome the money taboo and having productive financial conversations about life transitions with your loved ones is not a panacea for family dysfunction. But it will go a long way toward making your financial and emotional lives a great deal healthier.

Disclaimers

Morgan Stanley is held harmless with regard to any legal or other issues that may arise from the advice and examples used in this book.

Tax laws are complex and subject to change. The information in this book is based on current federal tax laws in effect at the time the book was written and should not be construed as advice on tax and tax accounting matters to clients. The content herein was not intended or written to be used, and cannot be used by any taxpayer, for the purpose of avoiding penalties that may be imposed on the taxpayer under U.S. federal income tax laws. Individuals should consult their own legal, tax, investment, or other advisors to determine the laws and analyses applicable to their specific circumstances.

Investors should consider many factors before deciding which 529 plan is appropriate. Some of these factors include the plan's investment options, the historical investment performance of these options, the plan's flexibility and features, the reputation and expertise of the plan's investment manager, plan contribution limits, and the federal and state tax benefits associated with an investment in the plan. Investors should also consider whether tax or other benefits are available only for investments in your home state's 529 plan.

Note from the Author

In order to maintain privacy and confidentiality, the examples used in this book are composites based on the circumstances and situations of a number of different individuals and families, not those of single individuals and families. Any resemblance to real individuals or families is coincidental.

Notes

Chapter 1

1. An estate is made up of all the things an individual owns, including, but not limited to, marketable securities, real estate, art, collectibles, antiques, jewelry, and life insurance.
2. A trust is a fiduciary relationship in which one party, the trustor, gives another party, the trustee, the right to hold title to property or assets for the benefit of a third party, known as the beneficiary. There are many types of trusts that I will define along the way.
3. A charitable lead trust is a trust that gives property to one or more designated charities for a specified period, and then, when the period expires, pays the remainder of the trust, if any, to one or more noncharitable beneficiaries (typically members of the trustor's family).
4. An executor is an individual, or in the case of a coexecutor, individuals, appointed by a person who makes out a will, to administer the estate of the person when that person is deceased.
5. Probate is the legal process by which a will is reviewed by a court to determine whether it is valid and authentic.
6. An estate plan is a comprehensive plan to manage, hold, and distribute assets in the event that the owner becomes incapacitated or dies. An estate plan should be created with the help of an attorney who is experienced in the law of trusts and estate law. Elements of the plan may include creating a will; limiting estate taxes; naming a guardian for minor children; naming an executor of the estate to oversee the terms of the will; creating and/or updating beneficiaries

on plans such as life insurance, IRAs, and 401(k)s; providing for funeral arrangements; establishing annual gifting to reduce the taxable estate; and creating powers of attorney and trust instruments to direct other assets and investments.

7. Yield is the income return on an investment, usually expressed as an annual percentage of the investment's current market value.

Chapter 2

1. Asset protection is a type of planning that is intended to limit creditors' access to certain property while operating within the bounds of debtor-creditor law.

2. Estate transfer involves the shifting of assets from a donor to a beneficiary in a way that will minimize the legal tax obligation of the donor's estate, avoid probate, or be part of the estate administration upon the death of the donor.

Chapter 3

1. Stock options are instruments that allow members of corporate management to buy company stock at a specific price; they are issued by corporations as part of their benefit programs. An underwater stock option is an option with a buying price (called the exercise or strike price) that is higher than the market price.

2. Restructuring debt is altering the terms of a debt agreement in order to achieve some advantage.

3. An IRA is an individual retirement account, a common tool used by individuals to invest their retirement savings; it provides certain tax benefits. There are several types of IRAs: traditional, Roth, SIMPLE, and SEP.

Chapter 4

1. A prenuptial agreement is a written contract between two people who are about to marry, setting out the terms of possession of assets, treatment of future earnings, control of the property of each, potential division if the marriage is later dissolved, and other rights that need to be addressed.

2. A family limited liability company is a special type of business arrangement, recognized by some states, that can serve a number of estate-planning objectives. Typically, and simplifying slightly, senior-generation family members create the entity by transferring property to the LLC in exchange for membership units. Often the property that is transferred to the LLC is expected to appreciate in value over the years. Senior-generation family members may then make gifts of some or all of the nonmanaging units to children or other family members, taking gift tax laws into account. As the property grows in value, the appreciation belongs to the person receiving the gifted units and so is not in the donor's estate at death.

3. A postnuptial agreement is a written contract between two people who are already married, setting out the terms of possession of assets, treatment of future earnings, control of the property of each, potential division if the marriage is later dissolved, and other rights that need to be addressed.

4. A life insurance trust is an irrevocable trust that owns a life insurance policy, often on the life or lives of the trustor or trustors. If the trust is a structured policy, it can serve to insulate the proceeds from estate tax upon the death of the insured or insureds. It is often used to set aside cash proceeds that can be used to pay estate taxes.

5. A gift tax exclusion describes an amount that can be given away without gift tax.

Chapter 5

1. Loss of principal means the loss of a portion of an investor's original investment.

2. A guaranteed universal life insurance policy is a type of flexible permanent life insurance with guaranteed premiums, offering both the low-cost protection of term life insurance and a savings element of permanent coverage to provide a cash value buildup.

3. The estate tax and gift tax exclusion for 2012 was $5,120,000. Under the law that was current as of the writing of this book, both exclusions are to be reduced to $1 million as of January 1, 2013.

4. A 401(k) is a qualified plan established by employers to which eligible employees may make contributions on a posttax and/or a pretax basis. Employers may make matching contributions to the plan. Earnings accrue on a tax-deferred basis.

5. A profit-sharing plan is a plan that gives employees a share in the profits of the company. Each employee receives a percentage of those profits based on the company's earnings and the formula of the plan.
6. Liquid assets are those that are easy to convert into cash. Nonliquid or illiquid assets are those that may be difficult to sell.

Chapter 6

1. Long-term-care insurance is a type of policy that covers nursing home care, home health care, and personal or adult day care.
2. A power of attorney is a legal document giving one person the power to act for another person. It is frequently used in the event of illness or disability, or when someone cannot be present to sign necessary legal documents.
3. A durable power of attorney is a power of attorney that continues to be effective even in the event that the individual who grants the power becomes disabled or incapacitated.
4. A temporary limited power of attorney specifies the particular acts that the attorney in fact may do for a specific period of time.
5. A healthcare proxy is a legal document that names a person to make healthcare decisions on behalf of another in the event that the latter person cannot make decisions for herself.
6. A living will is a legal document that sets out the medical care an individual wants or does not want in the event that he becomes incapable of communicating his wishes.
7. The Health Insurance Portability and Accountability Act, or HIPPA, provides the ability to transfer and continue health insurance coverage when someone changes or loses a job, mandates industrywide standards for healthcare information through electronic billing and other processes, and requires the protection and confidential handling of protected health information.
8. A successor trustee is the person or institution who takes over the management of a trust when a prior trustee ceases to serve for any reason.

9. A makeup provision is a clause in an agreement that allows additional monies to be paid out to make up for previous larger or smaller distributions and therefore provides for an equitable division and distribution of estate assets.

Chapter 7

1. A special needs trust is a trust that, if properly drafted, allows a physically or mentally disabled or chronically ill person to receive income without reducing her eligibility for the public assistance disability benefits provided by social security, supplemental security income, Medicare, or Medicaid.
2. A trust with generation-skipping provisions is one in which the assets are passed down to the grantor's grandchildren or more remote descendants, skipping one or more intervening generations.
3. A flexible trust is one in which the trustees, the people who manage the plan, can decide who will receive the money, from an agreed-upon list, and how the money is to be shared.
4. Offshore trusts are trusts created and administered under non-U.S. law; they are often used to provide advantages in terms of protection from creditors.
5. A fiduciary is an individual or entity that is in a position of trust or confidence to another, and as a result has special duties created under law to act only in a way that is consistent with that person's best interests.

Chapter 8

1. A Section 529 plan is a plan that allows certain tax benefits for the funding of qualified higher education expenses at qualified educational institutions. They come in the form of savings plans that are not linked to the actual cost of tuition and prepaid plans that are linked to the actual cost of tuition. They are issued by states and are municipal securities, and are composed of underlying funds that invest in various asset classes.

Chapter 9

1. A qualified personal residence trust is a special type of trust used to transfer the grantor's residence out of his estate at a reduced gift tax value.

Chapter 10

1. A custodian account is an account created at a bank, brokerage firm, or mutual fund company that is managed by an adult for a minor who is under a certain age, usually 18 or 21, depending on state law.

Index

About the Author

Lori R. Sackler is a financial advisor and senior vice president at Morgan Stanley Wealth Management, where she leads the Sackler Group. Her team is dedicated to successfully guiding individuals and families through life transitions. Sackler is a Certified Financial Planner®, Certified Investment Management Analyst®, and nonpracticing Certified Public Accountant®. She is also the creator and former host of the radio show *The M Word* on WOR in New York City.